Tough
Mercy

Lost in despair, we found ourselves at the orphanage.

By Ted Chandler

Dear Dan,

Thanks so much for sharing my story —

Now — Go write your own!

Best wishes,
Ted Chandler

Published by Baptist Children's Homes
Of North Carolina, Inc.
Thomasville, N.C. 27360

Baptist Children's Homes of North Carolina, Inc.
Box 338
Thomasville, N.C. 27361-0338

Copyright © 1990 By E. Ted Chandler, M.D.

First Edition 1990

Library of Congress Catalog Card Number: 90-080163

ISBN 0-9625827-0-0

Printed in the USA By
Faith Printing Company
Taylors, S.C.

To Fran
With Love

Acknowledgements:

This work is the product of an almost lifelong journey, first as an orphan, then in the orphanage, and then ever deeper in a commitment as a member of the board of trustees. There is no way I can list all the wonderful people who have led and accompanied me on this journey.

First, my wife, Fran, who went without a husband for the time required to write. Her help is inestimable, for we shuffled papers, ideas, memories, pictures and words so closely that we were as one.

Those who pioneered the way and those who paved the roads deserve, not only acknowledgment, but profound gratitude. I am especially grateful to those who read the initial effort and generously offered editorial suggestions: Norman Jameson, John Chandler, Cal Chandler, Lois Edinger, Allen Carroll, Julia Simmons, Bryant Kendrick and Jim Wofford; and to Sally Hart who typed each of several drafts.

A special thanks to Cleve Wilkie who has written of his orphanage experiences in an engaging manner.

Dedication

To orphans throughout the ages, and to those who gave them hope, even when despair was at hand.

Foreword

The ritual repeats every first weekend in August. From across the country, and occasionally from beyond America's borders, they come. By the hundreds they greet friends, talk about the old days and generally offer thanks for a time in their lives when somebody took them in, healed their wounds and made life palatable.

The ritual is Homecoming Weekend at Mills Home, part of the Baptist Children's Homes of North Carolina, a venerable institution which has operated out of Thomasville since the first child was admitted on Nov. 11, 1885.

For many of the homecoming crowd, Mills Home will forever be The Orphanage. Call it Mills Home, or BCH, or a myriad of other names, it is, to many, simply The Orphanage, a place of roots and wings, whippings and comfortings, pranks and tears, worship and love, justice and mercy. Especially mercy. And most especially, love.

Orphanage life was tough. Love was tempered with justice, but justice was tempered with mercy. Tough Mercy. It was the Orphanage way of doing things, especially in the days when three or four hundred kids roamed the lofty knolls of the Mills Home campus.

Ted Chandler received ample doses of tough mercy. His was a journey not uncommon to thousands of boys and girls who had lost one or both parents. Talk to alumni who gather on those hot and humid August weekends, and the common thread of Ted's friends of the 30s and 40s is thanksgiving for toughness and mercy. It is that combination that draws more than a thousand of them back each year.

Ted Chandler's *Tough Mercy* is a 10-year labor of love. Written as only one who has "been there" could write it, Dr. Chandler has woven a tapestry of nostalgia based on meticulous research, interviews and a sharp memory of his growing up years as a child of the Depression.

If life is a series of tests, then *Tough Mercy* gives graphic illustration of the tests or rites of passage that Ted and his brothers, John and Cal, went through. *Tough Mercy* is one man's story, but it is Everyman's journey.

Tough Mercy is more than a history of the Orphanage during the Depression and early years of World War II. It is a narrative recounting one of America's most difficult periods. Life in America changed about the time the face of child care began to change. Mills Home initiated a series of transitions in the late

1940s just as America began to experience the great post-Depression, post-War boom.

Dr. Chandler touches a nerve in us all. Life at the Orphanage was an ingenious way to both adapt to and beat the system. Didn't we all try to do that in childhood? At Mills Home, if you didn't eat your greens, you stuffed them in your pocket and then threw them away. The chord of identification is sounded and we recall what it was like when we grew up. That is the appeal of *Tough Mercy*.

So, join us in this journey. Visit the Pig Palace, the Valley, Hamby Creek and the Church. Walk with Ted in his landscape of suffering, rescue, joy and victory. See on his palate the hues of toughness and the shades of mercy.

Share with the orphanage kids in their games of "bringing in" and "muffin" and "bum bum bum." Sneak out at night so you can sit on the front porch of your favorite girl, even though you would surely get caught and have to kill 300 flies as punishment.

Ted Chandler writes with empathy and humor. Just imagine the boy in Simmons Cottage who "found a flare along the railroad track and set the thing off in his pocket by rubbing it during Sunday morning services." Or the "pecking order" which demanded certain initiation rituals, one of which involved blindfolds and that same railroad track hard by the campus.

Ted Chandler left the Orphanage nearly five decades ago. But in a real sense he has never left. As *Tough Mercy* is being published in 1990, Ted has just completed a term as Chairman of the Board of Trustees of the Baptist Children's Homes. He married the girl he snuck out at night to meet, and still finds in her a "glory of surprise," just as he did when he first kissed her on her front porch.

You will laugh and perhaps even cry as you read *Tough Mercy*. As Ted says about his days at the Orphanage, they "showed us how to drill through mud and water for oil, how to sift through silt for the gold, and to chip and hack through stones for the diamonds within."

For thousands of children, the Orphanage has been the Mother Lode. For it was there that they discovered what tough mercy was all about.

Dr. Michael C. Blackwell
President
Baptist Children's Homes of North Carolina
January 1990

Table of Contents

1

Arrival

In January 1934 my two brothers and I rode all day in a cold drizzle wedged together with our belongings in parcels. John was ten years old, Cal eight, and I was six. In the glare of lights at journey's end we rumbled over a railroad crossing and through brick columns entered the orphanage. Charlie Rice, our half-brother-in-law, stopped the flatbed truck, pulled a letter from his shirt pocket, lit a match, read out loud, and rolled down the truck window to toss out the burned stem. In the pale fog the truck lights ghosted streams of boys and girls in sweaters and belted coats leaning against the wind, flush from the cold walking. The faces of two boys hung in the truck window.

"Can we help you, mister?" asked one boy, blowing on his hands and speaking through chattering teeth. The other looked past Charlie Rice who puffed away at his pipe.

"Those must be new boys," the second boy's face said.

"You, boy," Charlie Rice pointed to the first speaker, "Where's Miss Edward's office?"

"Why, Mister, you're sitting right at it. It's right there."

1

He pointed. "There's Miss Hattie now, coming from prayer meeting."

The boys went running toward a short, plump woman with graying bobbed hair and puffed cheeks rosy in the cold. "Miss Hattie, Miss Hattie," they called out, "There's some new boys, there." They pointed at us.

Miss Hattie, Director of Mother's Aid, who had visited us in our other life, now welcomed us, and asked that we follow her into the low brick office building. We entered a long darkened hallway, passed closed half-glass office doors with painted names, R. D. Covington, Treasurer; Eulalia Turner, Lady Manager; Sallie McCracken, Secretary; Archibald Johnson, Editor, Charity and Children; and I. G. Greer, General Manager.

We clutched string bindings on bundled belongings and followed Miss Hattie to her basement office. There she began our adaptation to orphanage life by explaining that we were to be quarantined for one week at the infirmary to let incubating disease burst out. The long trip, new people, strange words, and a new place, swept me with a bewildering sense of fright and loneliness.

Charlie Rice bade us goodby without emotion, giving each of us a quarter and telling us to "be good". A light snow had begun. We piled into Miss Hattie's car for the ride to the infirmary, a large, three-story building in an oak grove. Dull light shone from rows of windows. Snow flakes reflected in the truck lights and the wind blew them against shiny black trunks of tall bare trees. The driveway circled around a fishpond. From a porch at the top of a tall banisterless stair light beamed down on the pond, showing bloated gold bodies nestled among dark leaves, bumping beneath a thin cover of ice. We trudged up the stairs, carrying our belongings across the porch, past empty chairs rocking gently in the wind, and into the building.

Inside groanings and whimpers of pain seeped from the rows of rooms that opened into long corridors to the right and left of the entrance. The odor of ether hung in the air and wafted from the door lentils and walls.

Older girls moved about in the corridors. Some carried ice cream on trays to soothe throats pained from having given up

2

their tonsils. Others hurried by carrying towels and balancing basins of water that sloshed and splatted the floor. Yet another carried a whimpering child in her arms. A pale girl, smoking an Asthmador cigarette, blew out a musty smell as she listened with silent gravity to a young boy with a bandaged hand. He told of his recent misadventure in which a friend accidentally whacked his thumb with a butcher knife. The story brought tears to the girl's eyes and she asked, "Does it hurt now?"

"Not much," he answered.

Miss Hattie asked for Miss Rucker. One of the girls said, "I'll go get her" and dashed up the stair at the corridor's end. In a few moments she returned, holding the hand of a tall pretty woman who swished up in her nurse's uniform. We were given over to her.

Miss Hattie said, "They have not had supper."

"Take these boys downstairs and get them some supper," Miss Rucker told one of the older girls.

We followed to the basement and in a neat dining room were told to sit at a wooden table with settings of plates, glasses, and eating utensils. Another girl joined the first. They rattled dishes and pots and soon brought stewed apples, pinto beans, sweet potatoes, thick slices of bread, and glasses of cold milk. Throughout they were giving us a good look. During the weeks to follow souls were bared repeatedly as we stepped upon each new landscape of orphanage life. To take the measure of the new boy or girl was not just natural curiosity. It was an orphanage way of life.

Following supper we were shown to our bedroom, a sleeping porch with six beds in a row. There were two other new boys in the room. We chose beds close to each other. But for me there was no settling down. My thoughts came alive. I missed my mother and the others from our former life. I strained at every creak, groan, footstep, and in my imaginings conjured frightening things in the dark. I whimpered, John said, "Hush up, Ted, Hush up."

But there was no hushing up. A spring had been tapped, far beyond the reach of sibling authority or even physical intimidation. The sobbing went on, breath after breath, until I fell asleep,

3

exhausted, awakened a time or two by the clanging of a steaming radiator.

About daybreak a small boy came to the door ringing a bell. "It's get up time," he said. I jumped from the bed and pressed my face to the window. In the darkness shadowy trees were outlined. The sky lightened as we dressed. With first light I saw a rolling land with tufts of trees bordering pastures on which a herd of Holstein cows grazed. The pastures were separated from tilled fields by wire fences. The land sloped toward a small orchard bordered by a wide creek, and beyond which woods stretched for a long distance. Close to the infirmary were rows of chicken houses with White Leghorns and Rhode Island Reds picking and scratching in grassless fenced lots. Before I could finish my look around the boy came along ringing his bell "It's breakfast time," he said.

We followed the boy to the dining room. In daylight the room was warm and low, and opened into a kitchen at the far end. In the kitchen a calm and serene gray-haired woman swung her head from side to side humming a light song as she worked over a metal table filling serving bowls with scrambled eggs and arranging limp bread on a sheet pan. She dispatched two girls, who carried the dishes and placed them near the center of three tables set with tableware and napkins for six at each table. Plates of toast and glasses of milk were added.

There were several children crowded at the dining room door pushing to enter. The walking wounded and those recovering from sickness forced ahead of new boys and girls, the boys clad in woolen knickers and denim shirts and the girls in woolen skirts and blouses. We newcomers had not yet had time to form even tentative rules of conduct for the circumstances of this new life. The others pushed and elbowed without malice, neither giving nor taking offense, all talking at once or silent at once as they forced the doorway.

At breakfast there were several adults other than Miss Rucker and the dietician; Miss Sallie, secretary to Mr. Greer, and a number of teachers, including Miss Olney, a tall thin wisp of a woman, also known as the Bird Lady, because of her knowledge of and

4

great effort toward educating orphans to the care and safety of "our marvelous feathered friends."

We sat. Grace was asked and food was passed. We new boys and girls stared too long at the sight with vacuous eyes. We moved with timid reflexes, taking too small portions to suit our hunger but, being under observation, we wished to make a good impression with our manners.

At seven o'clock a great bell called out from a distance, its deep voice repeating, "come now, come now," setting off a flurry of activity. About half of those eating at the dining room tables grabbed books and coats and satchels and hurried from the building to school.

After the scholars left my brothers and I were sent in the care of one of the infirmary girls to the sewing room to be measured for orphanage clothes. Outside, boys and girls sallied forth from other buildings nearby, spilling into a horseshoe road, laughing and joking and linking arms together, hurrying to school or to appointed places of duty.

The sewing room, a long low brick building with a wooden porch, was only a short walk away. The inside was one large room filled with girls in straight-backed caned-bottom chairs feeding cloth through Singer's jaws. Their feet peddled furiously. At strategic moments they flashed scissors, snipping connecting threads, and laid aside finished garments of underwear, khaki short pants, denim shirts, overalls, dark brown knickers, and long pants of olive green.

We were given over to a smiling, brown-haired woman in a long dress. She was draped with a soldier's sash stuck with needles with flowing threads, pins and loops of thread with thimbles hanging loose. Around her neck dangled a measuring tape, its free ends flapping as she walked. From her hair, just above one ear, a pencil protruded.

She said, "I'm Miss Wright. I've been expecting you boys." She picked up a tablet of paper from a padded table on which lay folds of denim rolled from a bolt. "Now," she said, "which is John, and Calvin? You must be Ted." She wrote on the pad. "Well, come along boys. Let's get measured and fitted for your new clothes.''

The girls, fresh and pretty and wearing bright colors, smiled and laughed, and looked up from their machines as we passed. Most had bright ribbons tucked behind ears and bows tied atop sparkling hair. We passed other girls working at cutting tables lighted by low hanging metal sockets with string pulls and bare bulbs. The girls reached to shoulder high racks, pulled out bolts of tight wound cloth and cut what they needed, dropping scraps in piles on a clean floor.

Miss Wright led us to one end of the room and behind a screen of denim draped over a wooden frame she measured arms and legs for length and waists and chests for circumference, jotting the numbers on her note pad. A peephole, created where the cloth screen overlapped, enabled me to watch the girls at work. Miss Wright brought us one piece underwear of thin, stiff white cloth cut with armholes but no sleeves. It fastened with a row of buttons in the front and in the rear had a slit that buttoned. I was fitted with short pants and denim shirts, John and Cal with knickers.

"These are your everyday clothes.'' Miss Wright said. We were fitted with other pants and shirts. "These,'' she said, "are your school clothes.'' And another set was for Sunday. She marked each item with India ink, "so that it won't get lost in the laundry.'' We returned to the infirmary bearing our new clothes.

After lunch we were taken to the first-aid room and instructed to sit on a bench "until the doctor comes.'' We looked into cabinets containing shining scissors, colored liquids in bottles, boxes of bandages, rolls of tape, and salves in jars.

The doctor, a tall man in dark clothes, bent over each of us, probing crevices, parting hair, pounding chests with bony fingers, putting the stethoscope to pounding hearts and blowing lungs. He searched for cooties, itch, and congenital weaknesses. We were declared physically fit and therefore no threat to others but we were to stay out our week in the infirmary to give contagion a chance to show.

That was the way we came to the orphanage, in the winter

6

of one of the middle years of the Great Depression, to a campus and farm of four hundred eighty acres of rolling hills thick with oak, pine, and dogwood trees. In Charlie Rice's truck we had entered the road to the boy's side. Another road entered at the girl's side and the two met, forming a large loop, called the Horseshoe. The seven girls' cottages, large, two-story brick buildings, were spread along the road to their side and the boys' cottages, also seven, were placed near their road. All the cottages were named after generous benefactors to the orphanage. The roads and cottages of each side were built on slight ridges with an area known as "The Valley" between them. The Valley, a major orphanage playground, occupied about a third of the campus inside the horseshoe. The other two-thirds was filled with a gym, library, an office building, and Mr. Greer's House. At the campus entrances a privet hedge ran parallel to the road. Beyond the road the railroad tracks ran east and west. Side roads ran from the horseshoe to the farm, poultry yard, laundry, dairy, and to a large building that housed a printing shop and carpentry, plumbing and cobbler shops.

There were more than five hundred boys and girls in the orphanage, boys and girls like us with one or both parents dead. We came from homes perched on hillsides, scattered along country roads, hidden away in mountain coves, located along the streets of small towns, and from mill villages. We came from Hickory Grove, Buffalo, Center Grove, Granite Falls, Cross Roads, High Point, Rock Springs, Sound Side. We came from Zion Hill, Mt. Moriah, Bethany, Mount Pisgah, and Mount Zion. We were sent from Baptist churches; Red Marble, Notta, Ivanhoe, Inez, Sweet Water, Paint Gap, Mildred. Each child, whatever his or her origin, represented a home broken by tragedy, disease, poverty, or violence and so on down the list of human woe.

Each of us lived somewhere else before coming to the orphanage. Each came from a particular dread, a despair. Whatever the antecedents of our orphanage days, the residual sorrow must first be overcome before we could become orphanage boys and girls. The sorrow began its thinning out when we transferred from the infirmary to cottage life. I was to go to the Simmons Cottage and John and Cal were sent to the Chowan.

7

Aerial view of Mills Home campus, 1946. — Photo by Stan Easty

2

Despair

Before our orphanage life we lived on Holland Creek Road near Horsehouse Mountain, Madison County, North Carolina. The mountain, rocky and steep on the sides, was flat enough at the top to serve the purpose for which it was named. During the Civil War mountain people, afraid of both Union and Rebel raiders, corralled their horses there, hiding them in a locust and poplar grove which sloped to a knoll of knee-high, rich blue grass. My grandfather, Martin Chandler, bought ten acres on top of the Mountain in the 1880's and built a house there. In 1913 my father bought adjoining land, giving a mule and one hundred dollars for a clear title to twenty-five acres more or less.

From the top of Horsehouse everything in sight made for grandness. The immensely wide view, the distant Blue Ridge, adorned with peaks of hardwoods, spruce, and fir, signaled freedom and unrivaled grandeur. From the top the exquisite and drastic contrasts of the seasons were vividly etched. But the chief features from the top were the light, the expansiveness, and the purity.

It was a sight which made my father, a man scarcely able to read or write, wax eloquent as he pointed toward the horizon across seven mountain ranges. "There," he said, "That's Craggy. The laurel grows high as a house there," and then, bringing his arm down, he pointed to our house. "It's like living up in the air, up here," he said.

Overhead a profusion of powerful, weightless, everchanging clouds towered up and sailed by, sometimes like ocean foam or piles of wool. Often the sky was dark blue, sometimes pale blue or violet. Up there everything made for peace, only nature could touch you. It was like a fortress, unassailable.

Because our land was steep and rocky, its bounty, if extractable at all, required backbreaking toil. A plot tilled for years was swiftly overgrown with sawbrier, blackberry, thorny locust, and thistle. If left untilled one season all trace of the plow was lost.

But the land at the top of Horsehouse was different. It was flat in contour, and the soil black and fertile from centuries of fallen leaves and rotted tree carcasses. There we grew magnificent corn, dark green pole beans, and deep red Wolf River apples so big that two filled a shoebox. We hauled the produce to the barn on a large wooden sled. We took the surplus to town and sold it for a few dollars. Money was scarce and carefully spent.

Shaped like a giant amphitheater with the tall mountains towering in the rear, our land had an open knoll in the center. On the knoll my father built a small log house. He was a good farmer but only a rough carpenter. Clear, pure water was fetched from a nearby spring which was famous because it had never gone dry. There among the cherry, plum, Hoover and Wolf River apple trees my brothers John, Cal, and I shared the experiences of our father and mother who pursued a life of fidelity, toil, and procreation.

There were wonderfully good times when Papa and we worked along, the heat of the cornfield rolling the sweat off us until the black soil's powdery dust caked us, and we looked at him and he at us and we laughed and rolled in the grass, because we were inky except for our teeth and the whites of our eyes. When the sun went down we went home and in the shade of the porch let

10

the cold water wash our heads and arms until our skin was numb and we looked clean again.

There were thoughtful times when he haltingly read the Bible to us or said wondrous, mysterious, proverbial things like, "He that would eat the fruit must climb the tree," or "The child is the father of the man," sayings which he had heard somewhere, sometime, and forgotten the when and where but remembered the wisdom.

Our farm was a wonderful place to spend a childhood. The days of summer blended with each other. We followed Papa as he worked the land. Our ears strained to hear when he spoke for he was a wise mountain man passing on his secrets to his boys. Secrets about when to cut the locust trees to get the best posts, how to use a reaphook on a slope all day without tiring, layering the wheat in neat rows to make it easy to tie the bundles. He showed us how to move the cattle along without spooking them, and how to pluck the eye of a squirrel with a twenty-two at fifty yards.

We trained our eyes as we caught the orange and brown salamanders and the slithering crawfish in the creek and kept a sharp lookout for the copperhead. When we tired we lay in the stubble of the cut grain, or among the daisies in the pasture, and listened to the silence, broken by the ever moaning wind as it undulated through the tall trees. We heard the shrill cree of a hawk as he swerved and dipped to avoid the sharp beaks of a flock of crows who resented his presence and punctuated their resentment with raucous caws as they flew as near him as they dared.

Wandering the woods we found caves with huge rock overhangs marked with black streaks which we swore for a fact came from Indians who camped and cooked underneath. We knew it for a fact because up by the high spring, the origin of our creek, almost at the top of our land, we found arrowhead flints which bespoke the presence of a goodly number, maybe even a whole tribe.

Papa was as vigorous at procreation as he was at farming. My mother, his third wife, was twenty when she married Papa and he was forty-eight. The two wives who preceded her

11

produced twelve children. Seven of them lived. I don't know what the other five succumbed to, nor what killed the other wives.

My father took in the grand beauty of nature's endowment and fused it with his goodness and country lore for the betterment of his offspring. But the tenuousness of life burdened him so after the death of his second wife that his eyes beheld only the hard, endless, dirty work of rearing four young children, Ralph, Kermit, Pearl, and Clyde. He searched for a woman of strength to share the load and to warm him during frozen nights when the wind blew down and sifted snow onto the bed quilts. He confided to his friend, Preacher Decatur Ponder, that he had searched the county over and found no suitable woman. He confessed that his wits were at an end. He was enlivened when the preacher advised that he journey to Yancey County and acquaint himself with the girls of the McIntosh family, especially Mamie, the middle girl. Mamie lived there with her brothers, Marion, Creed, Sherman, Grover, and Floyd, and sisters Florence and Augusta. The father had died years earlier, leaving the mother to manage their farm with her sons and daughters.

My father's name was Baxter Harrison Chandler but when people spoke of him it was shortened to Bac Chandler and always voiced together. He met Mamie and in a short time the acquaintance was cemented by his powerful persuasion and she agreed to marry him. They married in secret in the parlor of the preacher's home on September 17, 1918, and straightway she went home, announced that she was now a married woman, gathered her belongings and moved to Holland Creek to take up her new life. Her brothers and sisters were delighted. They were a spirited, adventurous crowd and except for Augusta, known to us as Aunt Gus, were planning to quit the farm for California in high hopes of reaping great fortunes.

My mother was a slender, pretty, brown haired mountain girl whose life among brothers and sisters had trained her well for rearing children of any age. Life at home in Yancey County was a level above that at Holland Creek, but neither was an advanced civilization. In the homes on Holland Creek, electricity, plumbing, radios, telephones, refrigerators, and indoor toilets were unknown. For baths, laundry, and dishwashing, water was hauled by the bucketfull and carried uphill from our spring. My mother chopped wood to fire her cookstove and to heat the iron water pot in the yard. She boiled the laundry, scrubbed it on washboards until the skin of her knuckles cracked, wrung it out by hand and prayed for the sun as she hung it on a wire stretched between two locust posts.

The logs on the outside wall of the house were not tight and, perched on the knoll as it was, the family lived at nature's mercy. When a cloud hovered and the spouts of heaven opened, the wind whipped and curled the sheets of rain until they fit the cracks and flowed through to flood the tiny house.

Such havoc had a way of disrupting the ordinary day, the killing and plucking of chickens, baking bread, patching clothing, and darning socks by kerosene lantern, growing and canning vegetables, preserving fruits, picking potato bugs and corn worms to protect the garden crop, making jellies and relishes, and tending the nasturtiums, hollyhocks, dahlias, and peonies that we nurtured to balance the toil with a sense of color and beauty.

The process of baby delivering was attended by midwives, some good, others not so good, but all without the newest medical wonders which were slow to reach up the dirt roads into the coves of backcountry Madison County. Dr. Locke Robinson was called if the case seemed out of hand but finding him was a mixture of chance and God's providence since he covered a large area on horseback.

Difficult labor, a limp baby, grave illness of all sorts was treated with prayer, herbal broths, and ancient folk medicine recipes. Infants died from bad positioning within the womb, mismatching of its body with its mother's anatomy, or infection from poor sterile techniques. Children were laid low and in some cases carried off by diphtheria, scarlet fever, or measles. Early death was commonplace and accepted with resignation. Those intimately connected with the case, families, neighbors, and acquaintances at large, were quick to place the blame on God "It's God's will" —instead of on ignorance, superstition, and being born before medicine's advances could give promise of recovery from

13

diseases which had not been thoroughly researched.

My mother threw herself into the care of her new charges with exuberance and vigor. She grew to love them and the young ones returned her love in like measure. Only Horace, papa's oldest son, rejected her. He considered her an intruder but he seldom made trouble as he was married and lived away.

My father welcomed his new bride by writing her name in the family Bible. Before long he saved a little money and built her a new and tighter house of wide boards milled from the trunks of giant chestnut trees slid down the mountain behind the heaving chests of straining horses. The new house was set closer to the spring above a grove of sour cherry trees. Soon the house was filled. The older children had babies to play with. There, in her new house, Mama did her work, stopping long enough to sit on the front porch and rock her babies and to look down the long V between two mountain slopes and wonder about the world beyond her own. As each child was born papa entered the name in the Bible.

Later, when papa got a little more money, he bought a new sofa to grace the living parlor and still later, during a trip to Greenville to sell apples, he brought home a green cuckoo clock for the mantel. It was an automatic marvel as it whirred and clicked and on the hour and half hour, day and night, sent forth a carved harbinger who gave notice of life passing, a message most notable in the winter when the family gathered in the parlor and the babies played on the floor before the fire. I sat there one cold night placing wood chips on the fire and before John could stop me had placed his new shoes on the coals and gleefully watched them burn.

My mother's record of child bearing was no better than the earlier wives. I was her sixth child, but only half of us lived. One baby, arriving early, unexpectedly, had died when my mother, alone in the house, lay still, afraid to move, under the fear that if she did she would die.

My successful birth brought Papa's count to eighteen, not a record in the mountains, but at the least a respectable showing. The local record was held by a family across the way, over in Yancey County. At the end of the count they had produced twenty-eight children in a three-room house. The back room was the children's room. They were inhospitable to strangers and unsociable with neighbors, preferring to keep their strain pure, untainted by the outside world. In the children's room they kept each baby isolated until the next was born, not allowing it to set foot outside until the new arrival pushed it from the nest. Then, toughened or not, it took its place in the world along with the brothers and sisters who preceded it.

Our land was at the end of Holland Creek Road, a two-mile long wagon road with deep muddy ruts in wet times and a rocky hard surface during rainless periods. Alongside the roadbed lay the banks of Holland Creek. The creek was named for its first settler, a Mr. Holland. At its lower end Holland Creek Road ran into the road to Asheville, thirty miles to the south.

In the summer the road was lovely with wild day lilies growing along the creek banks. Groves of tall birch trees grew close to the road creating a canopy of limbs and gloomy dark tunnels which shielded the land from the warmth of the sun. Snow fell on Holland Creek when it fell nowhere else and those dark tunnels kept it around forever, creating a passage impenetrable to horses and wagons. We were isolated during those times.

Good neighbors, the Bob Mathis family, Joe Marion Mathis, Rellie Ponder, Jim Byrd, Starling Ponder, and old man Joe Chandler, lived within walking distance. Their friendships softened the sense of isolation and in times of crisis, death, or serious sickness, the meaning of neighborliness came to full fruit.

There were good times when the neighbors assembled with a communal spirit to build a house, to shuck a barnfull of corn, to quilt and gossip, or to have "dinner on the grounds" at church. We circulated among the tables smelling the rich beef and pork roasts, the yeast breads, and vegetables of all sorts. We eyed the six layered stack cakes and marveled at how each layer rode on a bed of moist red sauce, the natural color cooked from the Hoover apple. We searched for a chance to snitch some small morsel, just anything to ward off starvation while we waited for the preacher to be done with much praying. We felt blessed

15

enough if the steal was made without detection. Afterwards we circulated and wedged our way amongst the grown-ups and ate until we feared we would burst, ran to play for a time and, starved again, returned to the table to gorge anew.

Our Holland Creek neighbors, for the most part, were like papa and mama, tough, resourceful, uncomplaining, and unyielding.

For three years I slept in papa and mama's bed drowsed and nuzzled to the warmth of flesh and safe from the fears of darkness. The sharing of their bed during that three-year period I expected to last forever. I had not known, or could not recall, any night spent away from them. My father was a kind, gentle man. He was lean in the awkward mountaineer style. His hands were rough, callused, big knuckled, and competent, a farmer's hands, but when he handled me it was with easy soft moves as though I would break. He had strong thick wrists and legs which carried him with confidence up the mountain behind the horses. He was known to be honest and forthright, the kind of man a boy was not ashamed to name when folks asked him who his papa was.

On Saturdays, if the work was caught up, papa carried me on his shoulders and John and Cal scampered alongside as we journeyed to Buckner's store. It was a rambling frame building with weathered brown siding entered through double screen doors flanked on each side by benches filled with men and boys who talked, guzzled cold bottled drinks, chewed tobacco, and smoked cigarettes.

Mr. Buckner carried a vast array of goods, enough that a family never had to venture from the valley to find the necessities. In the spring of 1930 Mr. Buckner made much of papa's health, remarking that his overalls fit too loose and his face looked thin. Such talk caused me to shiver with fear that something was going to happen to my papa. It was true. His flesh was melting away. A goiter in his neck caused his eyeballs to bulge and his mustache, once trim and neat, to look weathered and scraggly. Soon his strong thick wrists thinned and his step faltered when he hitched the plow or walked Old Doc, Coley, or Jakelag, our horses, up the trail to the field on top of Horsehouse.

That summer we continued to traipse over the land and to listen to the beckon of our father but his eyes betrayed the change in his body. He looked frightened much of the time and the simplest tasks, taking a souper from a beehive or sitting to snap a dishpan of pole beans, were done with trembling of his hands. His calm demeanor was disturbed by a sense of impending doom, inevitable in Grave's Disease, caused by an overactive thyroid gland.

About the time for harvesting the Wolf River, Hoover, and Winesap apples, a series of bewildering events occurred. Papa seemed to sense clearly the reality of his plight. Life was a struggle for him. The changes in his body were undeniable. He needed to be nearer the doctor and wished to have his family closer to church and school. He was beset with an acute sense of desperation.

In a transaction that to this day evokes mystery and conviction that he knew not what he was doing, my father sold our farm. He received no money, only a note promising future payment from a man, who, like he, was short of cash, but wanted the land desperately.

Papa moved us to an old shack at the head of Walker's Branch. The shack was nearer the doctor and the store, but in its best days it provided little comfort to those housed within. After our fateful winter there it was considered uninhabitable and was used as a tobacco barn. We were to build a house in the spring, on a piece of land that to this day has no natural beauty to recommend it, only scraggly pines and eroded banks and gullies which look at each other with no promise of the grandeur of mountain land like our Holland Creek farm. Land that evoked tranquillity in the anxious, peace in the troubled, and strength in the weak.

Papa's sense of desperation deepened; mama was with child and delivery was expected in the early spring. The winds and snows were furious that winter. They bore down in a series of crises that would have tried the wits of a well man; wood to be cut, hauled, and split for a fireplace with an unquenchable hunger, food for three young ones, and a wife with child. My father did what his body would allow him to do and made it until late winter. There were days of lengthening time when the sun brought a message of the inevitability of spring and there was hope that the worst was over. A late winter storm dashed all hope. Papa was chilled during the exposure and pneumonia developed. Dr. Robinson was called and came but pneumonia in that day was regarded as a friend of the old and infirm for it ended their travail. For papa, who was sixty-three, the story would likely have been different had his body not been weakened by the Grave's disease. As it was the pneumonia in its natural course reached a crisis stage in six or seven days and the outcome would be determined then. We waited.

A pallet was fixed on the floor near the hearth to allow the warmth of the fire to soften the hard chills. Whiskey and honey quelled the coughing spasms. Those special times we had shared in bed came to an end. Before the pneumonia papa had often pulled me to him in a tight hug as he sat on the sofa. I sensed the special feeling of those moments and to watch him, feverish, coughing, and delirious on the pallet began a work of sadness within me. The pneumonia reached the crisis stage and we waited still longer but papa's body was weakened beyond recovery. The illness lingered causing his heart to fail and his breath to come in rattles. In the early spring he died. Two days later the baby was born. John was seven, Cal five, and I was three.

Papa in his desperate acts had expressed the struggle between soul and body, a struggle which moved sometimes in giant strides and sometimes at a tardy sluggish pace, but slow or quick, ever sure and certain; it moved inexorably toward death.

For my mother the severance of death, the ritual of its meaning, was interpreted in long sweat drenched nights and days that demanded action. Decisions had to be made. A casket had to be obtained. Fred Holcolm had one which he had made for himself but he sold it to Mama. There was room at the top of the hill where the babies were buried, near the grave of Martin Chandler. Men from the church dug the grave. The weather was bad. The casket was carried to the foot of the hill on a wagon and then transferred to the shoulders of men who carried it up the hill.

When it was all done Mama offered her last twenty-five dollars to Dr. Robinson for his attendance during Papa's sickness. He refused it, telling her that she would need it more than he. She sent the same twenty-five dollars to pay the mortician. The messenger stole the money. We watched as the world we knew faded. Surely, we thought, this is all that can happen. We watched with disbelief and hopelessness as an older family member came in our house, lay claim to and forcibly took, the family Bible, the cuckoo clock, and the sofa. Even the special things which papa had scrimped money to buy and which had added so much to our lives were now gone.

For Mama it was a time when death and life were strangely blended. Life took the gaunt and grisly form of death but death assumed none of the glow and hue of life. The good life we knew gave way to the evils of disease and dying. The secure boundaries of my mother's existence were hammered away by the blows of harsh reality: the loss of land, the loss of neighbors, the loss of familiar sounds, and the loss of warmth from her own hearth. But it was a certain fear, a dread which corroded the core of her being: the dread of life without my father.

A time of new life that should have brought joy delivered only dread to my mother. Homeless, penniless, no husband, three young boys and now a new baby to fend for. She was buried beneath the weight of dread and despair. She felt her body grow nervous and dark, her spirit broken.

She was committed to a mental hospital.

We watched but did not understand, for we were too young. We only knew what we felt. It was as though the two of them had died. We were now orphans. Of course we had no concept of the word but the events which had dragged us to this state were prophetic in their ultimate meaning. They set in motion another series of events which would not have been had life continued as it was.

In our community there was intense debate over what to do with three young boys, left orphaned. The baby, named for his father, Baxter Harrison Chandler, and called by his initials, B. H., was taken by Aunt Gus, Mama's sister, who had come

19

to help with the birthing.

Aunt Gus lived with her husband in Black Mountain, some fifty miles away. She was the essence of sanity in a world gone mad, the picture of unreserved confidence. A farm girl, now living in town, she preferred bright yellows and reds for her skirts and blouses. These brought out the beauty of her pretty face But it was the piercing look that belied the softness of her eyes for it cut through the facade of pretense as surely as if it were the edge of a knife. Once made, her judgments and decisions were delivered with a sharp sparkle of wit and a deep throated country laugh. She was childless and loving. She was glad to have the baby.

The break-up of our family, the separation from our land, not only wrenched our hearts, but also closed a book of annals recorded in concrete terms of personal and communal meanings. Our landscape was enlivened by a sense of history written by us and the loss was not unlike that of a tribe driven from a homeland it occupied for generations.

The debate over our fate was considered settled when Charlie Rice, the husband of Code, papa's oldest daughter, agreed to add us to his family of six children. They farmed two or three acres of mountain land, growing tobacco as a cash crop and a profusion of vegetables for their own use. Their cattle grazed an additional forty acres and their pigs rooted and wallowed in a pen by the smoke house.

The idea of adding three more mouths to their table was probably Code's. She was a warm-hearted country woman who tackled every kind of work and wrestled with it in good spirits until it gave quarter. She set a bounteous table and her large frame announced that she ate well. She encouraged us to do likewise and we did, for the shadows of the winter past had kept us lean. I remember eating fresh strawberries for the first time that spring and marveling at the succulent taste.

Much of the management of the Rice's farm was left to Carlie, the oldest son. The father, Charlie Rice, had a yen for travel and took jobs logging timber from mountain slopes in West Virginia. He came home two or three times a year to check on his family but the daily affairs were left to Code, Carlie, and all others old enough to work. At three and one-half years of age I was considered old enough to be a water boy. My job was to carry lard pails filled with cold spring water to those hoeing corn or tobacco in the fields. The lids of the lard pails were balky and hard to get on and off. Small problems loomed out of proportion and in frustration I cried and cried, missing my daddy who had lavished such special attention on me and who would have gotten the lid off for me. At times the sense of his loss made each pailful weigh a ton and I trudged along the rows like an old man. As it was, the lard lids birthed a resourcefulness in me for I found they could be beaten into submission with a rock.

Some of my memories of those times are vivid, others time has faded, many have been pieced together and enhanced by what Aunt Gus and others who lived on Holland Creek or nearby have told me. Aunt Gus had visited often when we lived at Holland Creek, especially when a baby was due or when there was canning to be done in August and September. She did tell me that I developed high-spirited, restless characteristics at an early age and that I was independent acting, preferring to run than come when called and to be dirty rather than be washed clean. In spite of my periods of melancholy and crying I was interested in many things and stored in my mind a picture when told how to do something or how something worked. These characteristics caused a bond between Carlie and me.

Carlie had absorbed all that he could about farming. He was steeped in books and advisory publications about raising cattle and growing crops. He was a whiz at grafting trees and had one apple tree with red delicious, yellow delicious, winesap, sheep-nose, and Hoovers growing on different limbs. He planted concord and muscadine grape vines and strung them on woven wire fences where we picked them in giant clusters, their taste so fresh and vivid that my mouth waters today to think of them.

We could have become good farmers under the tutelage of Carlie who later developed a model farm in a beautiful setting on the bank of the Cane River in Yancey County, but it was not to be. I spent six months of threatened existence there, threat-

21

ened by the antics of the youngest Rice boy, Bunch.

Bunch and I were close in age and both built stocky with thick chests and short legs. Beyond that the resemblance paled. I was quicker in my movements and distinguished by a face full of freckles and a head topped with cotton white hair with a prominent cowlick.

Even at four years old I was picked at by grown-ups who enjoyed having fun with me. Bunch was a first-class bully. Early in our stay at the Rice's he jumped on my back, locked his legs around my waist, slid his arms around my neck, half-strangling me, and demanded that I ride him. He was stronger and I gave in. The next day he did it again and it then became as regular as eating or sleeping. I hid in the rows among the tobacco stalks or in the corn fields. Sometimes I dropped into the creek among the roots of a locust tree or took off running to the tobacco barn where I climbed high in the rafters trying to escape his clutches. I stood in the horse stalls until the ammonia stifled me. He stalked me, searched out each hiding place, flushed me like a covey of quail and then triumphantly jumped on for his ride.

At night I dropped into bed utterly weary, slept hard for an hour or two and awoke unable to breathe as though a heavy weight was bearing down on my chest. I lay awake, sweaty and with heart pounding watching the day come. As birds cheerfully announced the newness of it I hated the time to dress, eat, and return to the field.

There was no solace. I was an obsession with Bunch and he a terror provoking tormentor to me. Code pulled him from me. Carlie manhandled him from my back. I became a cry baby. What could I do? He was stronger than I. My heart became wicked and my head devised schemes against him. In my heart I was a murderer. Abruptly it was all lifted from me. It was decided that I should go to Black Mountain to live with Aunt Gus. I was flushed with joy and could think of no place I would rather be, except perhaps Holland Creek with mama and papa. A year later John and Cal were finished with farming and we were reunited. Now we lived in town.

Aunt Gus, Aunt Florence, and Mamie, the Chandler boys' mother.

View from our Holland Creek Farm.

23

3

Layover

When we assembled in Black Mountain we swapped the splendor of distant vistas, solitude, and isolation of Holland Creek for a world that moved fast and was filled with its own splendors: electric street lights, paved roads, telephones, radios, cars, and noise. The melancholia of our spirits was not likely to last in a world so new and so wondrous. We were dazzled.

The Rices were our first great benefactor. Aunt Gus and Mr. Brackett became our second. They lived in a large, frame, two-story rented house on Cherry Street near the center of Black Mountain. Perched on an embankment above their street the wide front porch of the house overlooked Potter's Store, Ann's Cafe, the bus station, Shorty Kincaid's Barber Shop, and Dave Jones Trucking Company. From the front yard we saw the railroad, the depot, the river, and, in the distance, a mountain range with a solitary house halfway up its main peak. Mr. Woolcott's Photography Studio and Mr. Wright's Grocery Store were up the street. Making friends and sinking new roots seemed possible.

Homelessness, a jarring reality of the times, filled the Brackett's large house with more voices, moving feet, and warm bodies sleeping on pallets. We four boys and the Bracketts made a sizable enough family but there were others. Raymond and Hazel Brackett, not yet out of diapers, were given up by their mother to the care of Aunt Gus. Mother McIntosh, came from Yancey County to live with the Bracketts.

Mother McIntosh's body, thickened from the many children she had born and weakened from the effects of a stroke, was kept going by the insulin which came in the mail from her son, Grover, a pharmacist in Uncle Sherman's drugstore in an exotic sounding place called Indio. They were our link to what seemed the other side of the world.

Mr. Brackett was the man of the house, but his voice was largely unrepresented in our routines. He was a valuable man in the town of Black Mountain. He worked for the town and knew where all the water and sewer lines ran, and where their valves were. He had full knowledge of the mysteries of boilers and motors that kept the water and sewage moving.

Aunt Gus had the deciding voice and hand in our comings and goings. Mr. Brackett breached this authority on one occasion, and only one to my knowledge. He came home drunk and for a period was obnoxious. Aunt Gus put him to bed, removed his shoes, washed his face with a cool wash and covered him with a quilt. She told him "You're a good man. Now go to sleep." That was that. Mostly he left home by the time the sun was up and came home after dark, steady, day after day.

The promises of Mr. Roosevelt to do something about the Great Depression made little difference to Aunt Gus. Like a general she took charge of the army of misfits. Her spirit was as cheerful as an eternal spring of sunny days. She set about the task of survival with a sparkling wit and no taint of resentment. She hired on at Pat McGraw's Cannery, over on Broad River Road, walking the two miles there and back, carrying an empty bag in the morning and bringing it home at night filled with dented cans of beans, corn, okra, and tomatoes. On certain days she sent us to the Red Cross Office to sign up for the free sacks of

26

flour and dried beans.

From the flour she made large, mouth-watering biscuits which we split open and covered with a thick layer of fresh butter from the milk of the Kicking Heifer, a Jersey cow of contemptible habits, kept on at our place only because her contribution was too good to give up. Tethered on a peripatetic stake in the back of the house she picked grass on the periphery of the town's land. Our garden, tended by all those of sound limb and large enough to wield a hoe, provided the other essentials of good eating. Aunt Gus fixed delicious, filling food with unexcelled mastery.

Our natural bent was to explore our new surroundings, to wander down toward the river, past the Gulf Oil tanks, giving off their sweet smell of spilled oil and the sharp whiff of gasoline, or to sit at the counter at Ann's and savor the cold sparkle of a soda, for which we occasionally owned a nickel, and smell the hamburgers frying, for which we hardly ever had the dime. But Aunt Gus was not one to tolerate idle hands. She sent us across the street to Potter's Store to find work.

Mr. Potter's Store, just across the street from our house, was the center of commerce in Black Mountain. He had two large store buildings, side by side, with an arched connecting passageway.

The one building contained racks of tomatoes, potatoes, bananas, apples in season, green peppers, corn, and other essentials of life. A few non-essentials, such as peppermint balls and chocolate drops, costing a penny each, filled a smaller special rack. Overhead shelves were filled with cans of Big Sweet snuff, boxes of Jinks candy, Morton's salt, Karo syrup, Dixie sugar, Penetro cough drops, canned goods, and Magic Cement glue. These were handled with a pair of long tongs maneuvered by Allie Cook, a short cheerful man who was Mr. Potter's right hand.

The other building contained the seeds, feeds and fertilizers. Huge stacks of burlap bags filled with Chesterfield and Ralston Purina hog, heifer, and chicken feeds were separated from the fertilizers by narrow aisles, just right for crawling and hiding. Bags of cottonseed meal emitted their peculiar musty odor and the golden dust that colored clothes and bodies an unhealthy yellow.

The men we had known before were cut to the long-shanked mountaineer pattern and sat down to supper in overalls and brogans. Mr. Potter was a man of town with his business suits, white shirts, ties, and slippers.

He held court over a continuous stream of men of all sizes and dress who came to the store. They spoke to him briefly as he sat behind a long counter of polished wood in the corner near the glass entrance doors. He extracted small pieces of paper from beneath the counter and passed them across. Money changed hands. The buyer peeled the slips apart, and smiled or spoke an oath. Most threw them on the floor, creating a mess. There obviously was a need for clean-up boys. We were hired. Our first job, other than on the farm, was in a gambling den. Mr. Potter and his guests were playing the baseball lottery game.

Mr. Potter had fought in World War I, been gassed and because of weak lungs contacted T. B. He had come to Black Mountain, famed as a convalescent site for tuberculosis, found the place to his liking and settled down. He moved in a quiet easy manner so as not to awaken the germs sleeping in his chest. He never seemed perturbed, perhaps because of two prized possessions kept in a drawer beneath the counter, a German Luger pistol and a blackjack.

Mr. Potter and I became buddies and as one buddy to another he showed me his toys. He explained how to load the clip of the Luger, how to cock it, and how to shoot. He wrapped the thong of the blackjack around my little finger, ''Not the wrist,'' he said, ''Some thug will pull your arm off.'' At age five I was fascinated by these instruments of power and in my imagination I righted the wrongs of thugs, robbers, and others of the same ilk, rendering solace to the unfortunate victims.

Beneath his calm Mr. Potter was tough and pragmatic. He ran for mayor and, when the vote was counted, was deadlocked with his opponent. There was talk of a runoff but Mr. Potter was against wasting money for that. He suggested to his opponent that they flip a coin and the winner take office. His opponent agreed. The coin was flipped and Mr. Potter won. Our standing in town took a giant leap. We were friends of the mayor.

Mr. Potter had also a bit of a boyish devil in him. To our young yearning minds, taught to respect rank and revere older folks, he suggested a novel way of getting rid of a rack of overripe tomatoes. Handling them like a grenade he taught us to lob them over the street, arching them at just the right height to clear the edge of the house. The target was Aunt Gus when she took the milk pail out to confront the kicking heifer in the late afternoon.

Aunt Gus sized the aerial bombardment just right. She streamed down the steps, milk pail on her arm, crossed the street and poked her face in Mr. Potter's. "You," she said, "the mayor, the very idea teaching these young boys such a thing. Be ashamed. Be ashamed!" He was ashamed, or at least deterred. He never suggested that again. Later, but not so much later that the steam was gone out of her, Aunt Gus opened our eyes to an inalienable bit of wisdom, "Don't bite the hand that befriends you. You boys know better than to do something like that."

Mr. Potter soon expanded our duties. He had two delivery trucks, one run by a white man and the other driven by Bo Gardner, a young black man. We were assigned to help Bo.

The main streets out of Black Mountain; those to Broad River, Montreat, Ridgecrest and Swannanoa, split into dirt wagon roads running along winding streams or dead-ended into coves close to unpainted frame shacks perched on hillsides. Along these roads hundreds of mountain folk, distanced from each other and from town, tended small garden plots, raising enough to subsist on, and kept a pig or two, a few chickens, and a cow. On Saturdays they walked to town. In Mr. Potter's Store they ordered staples, fertilizer, seed and livestock feed. Mr. Potter could now boast of three new delivery boys, such as they were. For our part we took this new responsibility to deliver the goods with the utmost seriousness. We looked to our new boss for instructions.

Bo was strong. More than once we had watched him trim to size a boxcar load of 100 pound bags of feed in no time. In a rhythmic swing he plopped each bag precisely where it was to go on the truck bed, his muscles glistening with sweat and his breath mouthing a song broken by grunts as he hoisted and dropped each bag. No problem seemed serious enough to cloud

29

his smile or disrupt his laugh. No problem, that is, unless it was this new charge he had, three young, inexperienced, maybe even ignorant, workers to supervise.

Bo had no time for laziness or wander of the mind or body. When the truck was loaded, he was ready to go and drove off. We were left behind a time or two. "You boys stay close," he would say, "when we're loaded we leave."

We protested, "But, Bo —"

"Don't but Bo me. That's all there is to it. You've got to learn responsibility sometime. It may already be too late." Bo would not allow sloppy work which had to be redone. "Catch everything as you go along," he would say, "backtracking won't do nothing but work you to death." We worked away as Bo toughened and maneuvered us. All the while he smiled gently.

Bo was a teacher, a man with an orderly inquiring mind. As he leaned into the chasm housing the engine of the old Ford truck his magic touch caused the engine to purr like a contented giant cat. He introduced us to the battery, the generator, the carburetor, the fuel pump, the water pump, the radiator, and then told us how the parts made a whole and how they worked together. He slapped his hands together in glee when he worked out a slight disturbance in the rhythm. "Listen to that, just listen," he would say. Out enthusiasm for riding with Bo brought us forth each day itching to get to work.

On one of those first days of our new work the itch was so great that, instead of looking up and down Cherry Street, we dashed across the curb and a car came within inches of killing us. The driver cursed violently and threw up his arms in anger. He had brushed death within a whisper, but he was angry because his car was stalled. For our part we didn't give it a second thought. We left him cursing as we scampered into the safety of Potter's Store. But the screech of those tires on the asphalt echoed in our minds and nobody had to remind us to be careful after that. We didn't dare set sail across Cherry Street without looking.

Six days a week we labored, positioning boxes of groceries in a precise arrangement according to the order in which we were to unload. Through the heat of summer we all rode with Bo. During the winter John and Cal trudged off to school and it was Bo and I who wheeled and slogged our way through the snow, ice, and slush of muddy mountain roads.

Most every day Bo planned our runs to arrange a break, stopping in the winter at Dave Jones Trucking Company where we sat around warming by the iron stove, kept stoked to a hue with chunks of shiny coal. In the summer, at the depot, we sat in easy chairs, grounded on the graveled floor, leaned against the sidewall of a covered shed which housed two ponderous mail wagons. In these two places we were introduced to Bo's friends, Hub Morehead, Dave Jones, and Gus Jackson.

There we got the news of the world. Sometimes their talk was about the depression. Tones of good humor and civility dominated the conversation. There was no bitterness or self-pity. They were suspicious of "pie in the sky when you die by-and-by" solutions. They gave ground to the possibilities of the New Deal with its WPA Program. But, generally, they commented in lighthearted banter, that, in the course of time, when it was supposed to happen, it would all improve. It seemed their philosophy that life flowed and ebbed in a manner predestined and beyond their influencing.

Hub Morehead, dapper with a neat, trim mustache and always dressed in a suit-coat with white shirt and tie, led the discussions. Arrayed against him on some issues and aligned on others was rangy Gus Jackson who wore a working man's clothing; tough, olive green pants, denim shirts, and brogans. Dave Jones, a burly man, blacker than the others, hunched his shoulders and cracked jokes. Their genuine good humor mingled with genial contempt toward authority in the church, business, labor and government. Their contempt overflowed on the miracle ideas espoused by various "salesmen" as instant cures for the country's ills. "A fool could see that won't work. You don't believe that baloney do you?" Hub Morehead would say, triggering an argument from Gus Jackson.

"Now wait just a minute, let's see what all the ramifications of that are," Gus would answer.

Besides politics they talked about music, philosophy, and morals. They commented on white men who failed to measure up to their standards, calling John Burnett, a local, a "dirty old man" as he slouched about town, stopping suddenly on the sidewalk and walking his fingers down his leg, as though scratching an itch, and at his foot making a sudden stab for a cigarette butt at the edge of his shoe.

They talked about baseball, drawing an analogy between that game and the game of life with phrases like, "in the wind up," "the big pitch," "only bunted," "a real homer," and "aiming for the big leagues." They spun humorous tales about people in the church who postured with unabashed piety on Sunday and became more ordinary on Monday. They were men who loved their children and wanted good things for them.

We listened. Like a sponge we absorbed their philosophy, not just information, but attitudes, ways of seeing the world that were to stay with us for years. On Holland Creek the conversation was the same that had been going on for decades. Someone was sick and he looked like he would die any moment. Someone else did die and everybody said the same thing about him, "My don't he look natural." "Bob Maring has a sick cow, likely has the 'bloat'." "The ground is too wet and the tobacco will probably get the blue mold."

These friends of ours were different. They had traveled. They had been to New York and Chicago on the train. The train and the shiny rails through the mountains linked them to another world; a world they were teaching us about.

The train was a new and different fascination to us. In the night the wailing whistle and clackety-clack of the wheels telegraphed the freight train's arrival and movement as it passed the crossings and thundered toward Asheville. Its wail aroused, for a moment, the melancholy which had consumed me the year before. But only for a moment. The joys of life in Black Mountain had erased those memories.

On snowy days excitement built as the engine strained to make the grade, the churning wheels losing traction, slipping on the slush. Giving a final, circular frenzy it topped the hill and bore down on the depot, emerging out of the clouds like a serpent. The engineer slowed the pistons and placed the mail cars opposite the wagons as neatly as putting a peg in a hole.

Under the canopy of a gray sky, spitted snow covered the black cinders and dark ground with a pristine coat that made the world look clean and pure. Wearing my uniform of brown coveralls and a floppy black hat which came almost to my eyes I looked like an urchin to the stately men and women eating in the bright lights of the elegant lacquered and brocaded dining car. In fine clothes they lifted their knives and forks with such grace that I was convinced they were all rich and famous. The illusion of going somewhere came often to me as I watched people ride the train and heard the conductor call, "All aboard!" as he checked the time and with a wave of his hand signaled the passengers aboard and the engineer forward.

On Saturdays, after the deliveries were all made and the trains all gone, we walked up the street to Shorty Kincaid's Barber Shop. He had become a part of the circle of our Black Mountain friends and on Saturdays he always gave us two pennies each, one for the offering plate at Sunday morning services at the Vance Avenue Baptist Church and the other one for our pockets. We would sit in the theatre-like leather seats at the front of his shop while he snipped, clipped, and doused his final customers. In the back, through a passage hung with a denim curtain he had a shower with hot water from a galvanized tank heated by a small coal-fired heater. There, for ten cents, you could soak your body with pumice soap and emerge from the steaming chamber gloriously scrubbed.

Shorty was a vision of male inelegance. Baggy pants and starched shirts sagged on his chunky frame and his uncombable red hair was unyielding to Wildroot Creme Oil or bay rum. But he always smelled good.

Life in Black Mountain suited us. There was a lot about it that we liked, but the debate over what to do with us was not dead. Back in Madison County, Preacher Ponder and Charlie Rice made application for us to be sent to the Baptist Orphanage in Thomasville. Before time marched far Miss Hattie, the Mother's

Aid lady, visited us. She was on a fact-finding mission to investigate our circumstances and determine if they were appropriate for us. To her mind we were suitably located for the short run, but for the long haul we would be better off in the orphanage. We were given three months of grace for that prophetic decision to soak in but, since we had no knowledge of what the orphanage was like, the time was filled with a new sadness. We didn't want to go. Mama didn't want us to go. Aunt Gus didn't want us to go. But circumstances, for some reason, were beyond their control and as the three months passed plans were made for us to go.

Once the decision was made Aunt Gus marched up the street to ask Mr. Woolcott to come and make a family picture. Mr. Woolcott had moved to Black Mountain from Florida. He was a corpulent man with a bushy mop of white hair parted in the middle. Behind his thick glasses were kind eyes and his smile was one of genuine gladness that he and you were there together in the same place. His frame fit tightly, barely, into the seat of a tiny Austin automobile, the other side brought into sagging balance by his equally corpulent wife. There was scarce room in the back for his large portrait camera and tripod.

Sweating in the coldest of weather, Mr. Woolcott pulled at his bow tie, shrugged off his coat and pushed up his sleeves. He positioned and arranged us in the front yard of the house until he was satisfied. He stressed to us the importance of every family having a portrait periodically to record their place in history at that moment in time. His words struck Aunt Gus with force and on our vacations from the orphanage each summer Mr. Woolcott came and recorded our place in history.

Finally a day was selected and notice given that we were to be packed and ready for pick-up by Charlie Rice in his truck. We made the rounds of our friends, telling them good-bye and being told by them that it was the best thing for us. In our hearts, we felt that it was all a lie and that the best thing for us was to stay there with them forever. But we were packed and ready on that day in January, 1934.

Ted, Cal, and John at Aunt Gus's.

Aunt Gus. The kicking heifer in the background.

4

Origins

The orphanage was begun fifty years before our arrival by John Haymes Mills, a tenderhearted man of extraordinary vision and tenacity. We learned of its history as it became our home. About four thousand others in need of haven, had found it there before us.

Henry and Ellen McNeill came by train a few days before Christmas, 1893, tags around their necks and in the care of two kindly conductors. Ellen was five and Henry eight. The train stopped after dark at Mr. Mill's house out in the country three miles from the orphanage, near the railroad tracks. Mr. Mills listened for the train whistle as it passed the orphanage entrance, and by the time the steam engine had covered the three miles, he and two gangling boys waited at the tracks waving their lantern.

Mr. Mills was tall and barrel-shaped. His eyes sparkled with enthusiasm and hope when told "Here are new children for you, Mr. Mills."

He lifted Henry and Ellen from the train and with the boys in front, lighting the way, he carried Ellen as Henry followed.

Martha, Mr. Mills daughter, took immediate charge, getting the children supper and putting them to bed. Early the next morning she took them to her room and they sat as she made her bed. From a dresser drawer she gave them each, as Ellen remembered, ''a bar of the prettiest peppermint candy I had ever seen.''

When dressed they went with Mr. Mills in the cold to hitch the horses to a big rock-a-way buggy. They lurched and shifted over frozen roads to the orphanage. Mr. Mills lifted them from the buggy and, holding each by a hand, led them into a girl's cottage, the Mitchell House. He turned Ellen over to Miss Naomi Judd, the teacher, and Mrs. Vic Swann, the matron.

''I was seated among the biggest bunch of younguns I ever saw. They were as quiet as they could be, learning their ABC's from a wall chart. I was only five, but I already knew mine,'' Ellen related. Henry was taken to the Durham House, a boy's cottage.

That evening Mrs. Swann bedded Ellen down in a room filled with other girls in iron beds. She kissed Ellen goodnight and left. Ellen burst out crying. Heads popped up everywhere.

Bettie Farrier came over and asked her, ''What's the matter little girl?'' ''I want my brother to come and kiss me,'' Ellen said. Mrs. Swann was called.

''You can see Henry in the morning,'' she said. ''Bettie you sleep with Ellen, and the rest of you get quiet.'' The heads vanished.

Ellen snuggled up to Bettie. Bettie asked ''Did you say your prayers?''

''No, I don't say prayers.''

''Don't you know the bad man will get you if you don't say your prayers.''

Ellen wasn't afraid of the bad man but she was terribly afraid of that strange, new dark, so she hugged closer to Bettie and covered her head.

Drowsily Bettie compromised, ''Well, you can say'em laying down this time I s'pose, but you've got to say 'em.''

Together they murmured: ''Now I lay me down to sleep.''

With the ready adjustment of a child Ellen was soon sound

asleep beside a warm friend in a kind, but alien world.

Mr. Mills met and overcame callous indifference, ignorance, prejudice, and hostility in his effort to establish an orphanage. Many locations were visited and rejected. In January 1885, a friend, Mr. Scarborough, called on Mr. Mills at his home. They discussed the orphanage into the night. Early the next morning they set out to see an eighty acre plot three miles to the east.

Mr. Scarborough, almost seven feet tall, and Mr. Mills, six feet two and over three hundred pounds, rode in a road cart, a two-wheeled vehicle with a single seat. It was pulled by Tar Heel, a spindle-legged colt that had carried Mr. Mills all over North Carolina in his search.

The site was known as Paradise Hill, so named because great crowds of black people came every August to sing, preach, and praise God in revival. They built a brush arbor on the highest point, beneath a giant hickory tree and near a generous spring of good water. At each corner of the arbor they constructed a wooden platform and covered it with earth and there set great fires at dusk. Their spirituals and preaching were heard for miles into the late night.

Mr. Mills bought the land and hired L. E. Peace to take charge of clearing the land in preparation for building a cottage for children. Mr. Peace was assisted by Ransom Oaks, a laborer, and three mules, Sandy, Samson, and Delilah, were bought to do the hauling and heavy work. Uncle Ransom, as he was called, was a faithful black man who sang "Pharoah's Army" as he worked. Once, while ditching, he came down on his great toe and cut it off, thinking it was a turtle's head.

Mr. Mills and Mr. Peace walked the acreage until they knew every spring, every tree, hillock, gully, and dip. Mr. Mills wanted a new kind of house; one for a family of twenty-four, with a school room, and rooms for sleep and play. Mr. Peace studied each plot of land, sketched its contour on paper and located the building in the best place, drawing in ground space for chickens and a cow. Mr. Mills insisted that the children in each cottage be like a family, each with its living quarters, cook house, and sustaining animals. He planned for an orphanage of not more than one hundred

39

fifty children living in six cottages, three each for boys and girls. The Mitchell House was a ground-level building for twenty-four girls but there were so many orphans that the first building for boys, the Durham House, built the following year, was a two-story house for thirty. Mr. Peace, a skilled builder with a natural talent for design, gave each new building its own character.

As cottages were built, those to the west, arrayed in a row with a dirt road in front, were for boys and those to the east were for girls. Those areas were known thereafter in orphanage language as the Boy's side and the Girl's side. A road, known as the horseshoe, connected the roads from the boy's and girl's sides. As the years passed Mr. Peace built along the horseshoe a laundry, sewing rooms, an infirmary, a printing shop, and an office building. A large grassy meadow, known as the Valley, separated the boy's side from the girl's side.

Most of the children were county-bred, and the orphanage boys learned to farm, tend livestock, and, in some cases, printing. The girls learned to sew, to keep house, and to cook. All were schooled in the essentials of reading, writing, and figuring. The boys learned to use simple tools and the girls easily mastered their assigned chores. But what was of special significance was the establishment of each child in a routine of life, a routine of work, play, school, and church. Essential skills, lessons, and habits equipped each child to get along in the world. But the children were not passive receptacles, and they shaped the character of the orphanage even as they themselves were molded by their collective experiences. Each cottage, beginning with the Mitchell, had its own character.

The Mitchell House was a rectangular brick building ninety feet long and twenty-four feet wide. The north end was a residence for Miss Judd, the teacher, and Mrs. Swann, the matron. The south end was a school room. In the center was the sleeping room, eighteen by fifty feet, with a fireplace at each end. There were fifteen iron beds, two girls to a bed, in space built for twenty-four girls. Across the road and facing the cottage, was the eating house, measuring sixteen by sixty feet and divided into four rooms, dining room, kitchen, provision room, and the cook's sitting room. The eating house was built away from the cottage in case of fire. The matron was housekeeper, house mother, and cook. She and the teacher lived there with the children, the chickens, and the cow, nurturing and teaching the children, and caring for the animals.

In 1893 when Ellen McNeill came to live at the orphanage there were five cottages, each housing twenty-six to thirty children, a chapel, an arbor for holding the annual meeting for friends of the orphanage, a printing house for publishing the orphanage paper, an office building, and a bath house. Two hundred ten children had grown up there and had gone forth to work, study further, or to form their own families.

Shared experiences, some good, some bad, some strange and mysterious, brought the children together into a family larger than that of the cottage group; it encompassed the whole. Grand and sometimes sad orphanage tales evolved as friend told friend about the special times and what they meant to him or her. Such stories began naturally enough for they were the stuff of life itself and sharing them made it all the richer. There were routine first-time experiences, how to sew, how to hoe, how to do multiplication tables, how fast you learned a poem, how to milk a cow, how to harness a team and work the land, and how to run a printing press. As time passed the orphanage became more complex, more self-sufficient, and new experiences were added in the process.

Ellen told about the time she was a water girl at the Mitchell cottage:

> "Every girl had a duty. I was water girl. The spring was about one hundred fifty yards from the cottage and several times each day I carried buckets of water for drinking or washing. One day a girl told me that the water bucket was empty and I grabbed it and started to run. I grabbed a bonnet at the door but it was someone else's. It was a rule that we wear bonnets whenever we went outside. The girl who owned the bonnet tattled to the matron, and when I got back I was sent to the school teacher. Miss Judd laid me across her lap and tightened my

41

drawers and worked on my behind with a hairbrush. I
thought I'd never stop crying."

The teachers and matrons were attracted to orphanage work
as though it was a missionary activity, and it was. They meted
out a lot of justice, sometimes tempered with mercy. The two
great laws: "Thou shalt," and "Thou shalt not" had little flex-
ibility. Water was carried from the spring in cedar buckets and
poured cold into tin wash basins for daily ablutions. It was a lick
and a promise on the hands and face during the week, but on
Saturday the water was heated and poured into big tubs and grime
was removed by dunking and scrubbing until shiny. Two buckets
of foot-water were carried from the spring daily and poured into
a small tub that stood in the corner of the porch — a mute reminder that all feet were to be washed at night. A common tub,
a common towel, for the last person it was just too bad.

Later a Mrs. Lilly sent enough money to erect a bath house
for the girls. A steam engine pumped hot water into a four by
six by eight foot tank where eight or ten girls soaped in luxury.
Water was pumped by hand into a hogshead on the second floor
and they rinsed by shower. It was years ahead of its time and
far more luxurious than many non-orphans had in their own
homes.

Ellen learned to sew, to keep house, to read, write, and to
figure, and later, how to cook. She became a kitchen girl. It was
up at four, summer as well as winter, shake down the ashes,
take them outside and dump them on a pile to be spread on the
flower gardens, and build a wood fire in the iron stove. She sifted
six quarts of flour, mixed them for biscuits and rolled, cut, and
baked enough for each girl to have two. At six she rang the
breakfast bell.

There were good times such as the visits of Mr. Mitchell,
the benefactor who had paid for the cottage. He came often and
brought news of the world outside as well as gifts which expressed
his love for the children. Ellen recalled his visit:

"When he came we would run to meet him. He was a
small man with gray hair and a white beard. He had never

married but we were his children. He took as many of us in his arms as he could hold. Tears would roll down his cheeks. We went on to the cottage and sat down with him. He asked us to sing. We sang, 'We'll work until Jesus comes and then we'll gather round. We'll work till papa comes and then we'll gather round!' At the end of each visit Mr. Mitchell gave the matron a dollar to buy us candy.''

Sweets were a Christmas-time treat except for special times when Mr. Mitchell bought candy. Sugar was kept under lock in the pantry and in Sunday School when the teacher counted through the thou shalt nots of the Ten Commandments and paused on "Thou shalt not steal," sugar was the item in mind.

There is no record of the orphanage having an ice house and I know of no official document stating the first making of ice cream but Ellen recalled her first taste of it:

"It was early spring and we were all itching to get out, to take off our shoes and start going barefoot. A cold siege blew in and laid a deep snow. The weather warmed and melted the snow enough that Mrs. Swann could push a small wooden wheelbarrow through a shoveled path to the edge of a small pond. With an ax she broke the ice, filled the wheelbarrow and carted it to the cottage. She laid out the ingredients according to a recipe for vanilla ice cream. The girls clamored to help and she assigned some to break up ice while others mixed the ingredients. She shooed the remainder to the study where they fidgeted and milled around in a carnival atmosphere. Soon the bowls were put out and filled, and we all filed out to a sunny spot on the south side of the house. We sat in the warm sun on a board seat and swung our feet back and forth through the melting slush and tinked our spoons in the bowls. We pulled each spoonful through the mouth just enough to make the tongue tingle in delight. Slowly we repeated it, drawing it out, time and time again, making it last just as long as it would.''

Each cottage had its own garden, flock of chickens, pig or pigs, and cow. The cows were distinct personalities. Some were brindled and mule-headed. "Old Horny" was one such. For the most part, however, the children loved them and could hardly wait till school was out (12:30 o'clock) and dinner over to run to the barn and get their cows.

The big girls and boys milked and the little ones grazed and fed the cows. Lush grass and wild clover grew everywhere, sometimes causing overeating and foundering. When things went wrong the grazers went into a huddle, diagnosed the case and then treated it according to their veterinary lore. A case of indigestion was pronounced hollow horn if the horns were cold; hollow tail if there seemed to be a vacuum in that member. If, after boring the former or splitting the latter, they got no results, they resorted to drenching with a salt water mixture.

Once old Horny was ailing and failed to respond to treatment. When she didn't chew contentedly the girls made a cud of dish cloths and coerced a boy, D'arcy Belch, to help force it down her throat. She soon began chewing.

The supply of milk and butter was not always adequate, for Beaut, old Moses, old Horny, and Cot were subject not only to doctoring but were kept from grazing in peace by boys and girls who took advantage of their docility and struggled aboard for short bareback rides.

Most of the doctoring was done by the matrons and teachers but in serious cases Drs. Bird, Julian, and Flippin were available. The only surgical case at the orphanage during those early days was the amputation of Peter Muse's leg when it was hopelessly crushed by a train. It had to be taken off near the hip without benefit of hospital. Drs. Julian and Flippin did it in the infirmary as helpers held the lamps and heated the water. Miss Cora Bronson passed the instruments. The boys kept the fires going. Although he hovered in the shadows for days after his traumatic surgical ordeal, Peter pulled through. A strange thing, when he began to get better, he complained that his lost foot itched!

Pete Muse was a popular orphanage boy and the story of his accident was printed in the orphanage paper, *Charity and*

Children, on January 20, 1894.

"Last Saturday while a heavy freight was climbing a steep grade, Peter Muse attempted to take a ride. He fell and his left leg was crushed. He was carried to the Infirmary, and the doctors cut it off. Peter has been with us several years, and has been considered a handsome, bright, and good boy. He lost much blood and is very weak. We hope he may recover. He bitterly repents his folly; but is cheerful and tries to take care of his stump."

To pass the time of recovery and to make certain that he didn't repeat such folly his teacher and matron presented him with a Bible.

"Master Peter Muse's Book
presented by
Miss Effie Cain
and
Mrs. S. W. Hall
Peruse this book with utmost care,
Each verse preface with a prayer,
Eternal joy in them you'll find;
Record in your soul the truths combined
Many days shall be added to your youth
Upon the observance of one great truth;
'Search the Scriptures' is a Divine command,
Ever cling to the Omnipotent hand.
Jan. 20, 1894."

Not long after the orphanage was opened for children Mr. Mills bought a giant bell and placed it on a tower. It called the children to breakfast, to worship, to school, and on occasion it told of a death.

Ennis Atkins was the first child to die. The other children were bereft. School was dismissed. The children gathered in groups and were too sad to play. A grave was dug on a knoll among a grove of sassafras, dogwood, giant oaks, and hickory nut trees, and there at the funeral Mr. Mills wept. Soon death claimed others, including Stella Lambert, a beautiful favorite with black curly hair and pansy blue eyes. Death often splintered families. There were five Perkins boys: Jacob, Fuller, Arthur, John, and Willie. Arthur, freckled and crazy about horses, often drove Mr. Mills around. His death was a great shock as well as a deep grief. It was probably caused by appendicitis.

There were four Belch children: Tom, Ella, D'arcy, and Quinton. Quinton was severely hunched from an accident which broke his back in babyhood. He was a victim of typhoid fever. There were others but as sanitation improved and the children became better nourished the number of graves in God's Acre grew at a slower rate.

These were sad times that disrupted the routines of work, school, church, and play. The memories took on a somber hue when the sad times were due to sickness, for there was no defense. Ellen lived at the Mitchell cottage with Fannie Sharpe, Eugenia Sharpe, Mae Ammons, Eloise Herring, Tola Morrison, Mattie Laura Blanchard, and others. Her special friend was Sally Price. They loved each other. Ellen told of Sally's death:

> "Sally Price was my best friend. We slept together. She was so smart I believe she would have grown up to be famous. About five o'clock one evening she went to make a fire and, when bending over, took a headache. She got bad off with it and through the night couldn't sleep. She asked me to go call the teacher. We weren't supposed to make a noise after we went to bed. I went and knocked on the door two or three times, but she was asleep and didn't hear. I didn't know what to do so I came back to bed. I told Sally that the matron was asleep and didn't answer. I wet a cloth with cold water and put it on Sally's head. When morning came, she couldn't set up. After breakfast the children got off to school and the matron went to see about her. Mrs. Swann called Mrs. Boone, and she went to fetch the doctor. But before he got there a fit come on her. Doctor Julian came in a little while and stayed all day. He tried to help her, but the fits got worse and worse, and about five o'clock that evening she died.

They let us go in to see her two at a time. She had three brothers, John, Jim, and Gomer. they were at the foot of the bed crying. They tried to locate her mother, but were unable to find her, and had to bury Sally without her mother knowing about it. She was buried in God's Acre — the orphanage graveyard.''

Ellen McNeill recalled a scary, mysterious time, the disappearance of Clarence Withers. It was a time when the orphanage became obsessed with fear and suspicious of strangers, a characteristic alien to its usual nature. Clarence was a surly boy of thirteen who lived at the Durham cottage. He was restless and nursed a yen to be on the road, a trait inbred in some men. Impulse was stronger than plan. The first time he carried his trunk and got four miles down the railroad. Mr. Mills helped him carry it back. The next time he went without the trunk. Mr. Mills met him at the Yadkin River and they came back together.

Mr. Mills assigned Clarence to work with Buck, a large gentle oxen bullock sometimes used for log dragging and heavy hauling but whose primary duty was to pull a large two-wheeled cart built on the style of an ancient chariot with ponderous oak wheels rimmed with steel. Where Buck was the boys were and they clambered on his back and filled the cart hoping for a free ride. Mr. Mills hoped that comradship with Buck and the other boys would sway Clarence but it never did. In his heart he yearned to be gone more than he yearned to belong.

The Durham cottage sat among a grove of oaks, bordered to the rear by an open meadow which ran to the Johnsontown road. The meadow was the boys' playground and the road which circled its edge was the entry to the outside world. During the late days of spring a large family of Gypsies in two wagons drove in from the road and set up camp at the far end of the meadow. Their brightly lacquered wagons with tools, pots, and pans strung along the sides irresistibly drew the orphanage boys and they came to gawk as their olive skinned visitors settled in.

The matrons and teachers were suspicious of the Gypsies and told the boys to stay away but the entreaty went unheeded. The pull was too strong. In the evening the Gypsies built a great bonfire of wood foraged from the orphanage land. Their women, heads bedecked with scarves of bright crimsons and deep blues, jangled as they scurried around, their arms flashing from dangling, tinkling bracelets. They were truly foreigners from an exotic land. Over beds of coals pulled to the edge of the bonfire they simmered and stewed pots of food which gave off a mouth watering spicy fragrance. The bland orphanage winter fare of pinto beans, Irish potatoes, thick molasses, biscuits, corn bread, and milk was no match for the enticing odors from the Gypsy cooking pots.

In the late evening the orphanage boys scurried home as the matron rang the come-in bell. They sat for devotions in the study-hall, messed around for awhile and then went to bed. They raised their bedroom windows and lay in bed or sat on window sills and listened to the Gypsy sound. Spirited music wafted upward from the campfire as Gypsy men plunked their mandolins and strummed their guitars. It was a mysterious sound, a rousing and summoning sound.

There were Gypsy children who kept to themselves, peeking with suspicion from the insides of their wagons at the light-skinned, bony visitors. They kept to themselves until Clarence drove up in his cart pulled by Buck. The Gypsy young were drawn to Buck and petted him as the orphanage boys timidly gathered around. A breakthrough came in the standoff when a Gypsy boy made friends with Clarence, trading him a small iron bell for the privilege of brushing and currying Buck. The friendship deepened. Clarence spent much time in the Gypsy camp.

Mr. Mills, home from his travels for a few days, visited the Gypsies and asked them to move on. They left early one morning.

Clarence moped around for days. He was scarcely able to eat, missed important details in his work, and was more surly than usual. Three days passed and then, late in the day, one of the wagons returned but stayed only an hour or two. The driver drove away in a great hurry. In the morning Clarence was missed when he did not appear for breakfast. His clothes were gone. The story of his disappearance ran quickly from mouth to mouth, was deliberately spread amongst the orphanage children, and was then given to everyone in surrounding neighborhoods so that the people there would be vigilant.

A search was considered but delayed. Mr. Mills was away again. For six days they waited with fearful fantasies and speculation. Clarence was likely dead for, after all, were not the Gypsies skilled in foretelling the future through communication with the dead? There was fear that they would come again and grab other children.

Mr. Mills returned, gathered those facts he needed, and headed out to search for Clarence. He stayed away four weeks, followed clue after clue and lead after lead but discovered nothing. He called a halt to the search and rode east to tell Clarence's mother that her boy was gone.

The mother was a gaunt farm woman who had been widowed by disease and had not remarried but had borne Clarence out of wedlock. She lived in a run-down tenant house on a cotton farm. When told about her boy she made no demand for details other than what Mr. Mills knew and as she spoke her eyes looked down and to the side but never to his face. "He warn't mine nohow," she said, "youns took him to raise. Maybe he'll come back some day."

About five years later, after Mr. Mills died and Mr. Boone became the orphanage manager, a Baptist preacher told Mr. Boone what happened. The mother lived on at the farm and one day while tending a fire, heating water for washing clothes, she was approached by the driver of a Gypsy wagon and asked for a drink of water. On her way to the well the woman glanced inside the wagon. A young man lay asleep. There was a vague something about him that interested her and she drew closer for a better look. He awakened. It was her son. The reunion was joyless but he decided to stay with her and did so for one year but then left and was not heard from again. The mother told the preacher, "He warn't mine nohow."

A teacher, Miss Kate Durham, told the following story about Mr. Mills:

"Back in 1894 Mr. Mills was on the orphanage grounds one night after the silent bell had rung and all lights were out. He went into the Watson building to get a boy to

49

drive him home. As he entered the dormitory he heard a boy praying. In the dark he saw the form of a boy on his knees offering the following prayer: 'Good Lord, we need a barrel of flour; and please send us a barrel of meal. We would thank Thee for a barrel of sugar and we need a barrel of pepper — oh hell, that's too much pepper'."

In 1934, when John, Cal, and I arrived there were about five hundred forty children in fifteen cottages. And so we came, each life reflecting the essence of a personal tragedy. Taken collectively our early impressions comprise a gritty American tragicomedy. For each of us life contained trust, puzzlement, skepticism, and innocence. Some had a look that wondered, but demanded no explanation; a look like our father had near the end of his days, that of being overwhelmed; the look of humanity come to the last ditch, beyond help or the hope of help. We came because we had to come. We were children. We came because a place had been prepared for us, a place of hope, by people of great vision.

Ellen McNeil

50

5

Belonging

I began life at the Simmons Cottage with a sense of bewilderment among thirty-four other boys from six to eleven years old. I cried a lot each night after we said our prayers and the lights were put out. Our cottage was near the railroad tracks and regularly The New Orleans Express blew its whistle and rattled the windows as it roared on its way into the night, the clatter of its wheels hammering home my travail.

The matron was Miss Ballard, a tall, thin, worn-out warrior with brown hair pulled into a tight ball. She presided over meals and devotions but spent much time in bed resting, oblivious to the fighting and bullying that went on. She was assisted by Mrs. Mellons, the dietician, and they each had a room and bath near the entrance to our two dormitories.

Our cottage was a two-story brick building entered at the second story through a porch at ground level. The dormitories lay to the right and left of the entrance hall; large rooms with white, iron-framed beds, white sheets and patchwork quilts. There were thin pillows. The beds, pushed close together, lined the long walls of the dormitories, leaving a narrow aisle down the center. At the aisle's end there was one bed smaller than the others with siderails. I was assigned to it since I was a new boy and small besides. The floors were of well-scrubbed oak. We swept them every day and scrubbed them every Saturday. Near each dormitory was a large bathroom with four toilets and a bathtub where we bathed two to a tub.

We went to bed at nine o'clock under orders from Joe Phelps and Edgar "Fat" Green, big boys. They enforced quiet. Someone always yelled, "Turn off the juice," and a boy near the door jumped up and darkened the room. Giggling, talking, bouncing on beds, fighting with pillows, and quiet crying continued until we fell asleep of exhaustion.

There was a lot of fighting and bullying among the boys, which established a definite pecking order and division into big boys and little boys. Everybody knew who could beat whom. I didn't like to fight, but there wasn't any choice sometimes. My first fight came within the first week. It was a cold Saturday in early February when all the boys were home from school. We were in the play area, a hard dirt ground graveled with sharp rocks south of the cottage. A group crowded around me pushing and longing to get a better look at the new boy.

"Where you from," one asked. The others quieted to hear the answer.

"Santa Claus brought me," I answered. I said it in all sincerity, for it was what Aunt Gus had told me. "Santa Claus brought you and was late because of a big snow." My birthday is December 27.

The response was immediate. They laughed, jeered and mocked, "Santa Claus brought him, ha, ha." They obviously knew where boys came from. I was on the verge of tears and was about to give in to them. But the playground roared like a rodeo and then the rabble closed in to taunt me. I knew it would be "cry baby" if I didn't fight that day and would continue thereafter until I did. I took down one boy with a tackle, pushing grit into my face like shrapnel as we crashed. Others jumped in until it was a regular melee with gouging of sharp elbows, shirts torn,

52

skin burns, and bloody faces. It ended when Mrs. Mellon's big form streamed from the kitchen and she twisted an ear or two and said, "You boys should be ashamed of yourselves." I was picked on a little after that, until I had two fights with bigger boys and beat them both. There were Queensberry rules of a sort obeyed in fighting: you didn't hit an opponent when he was down.

We lived a communal life with few exceptions. But, our personal lockers were inviolate. The wooden lockers lined the walls of the playroom in the basement and were not only for hiding our marbles, string, stones, pocket knives, coins, secrets, and treasures, but were also seats during bad weather when we spent much time there. One box, which I don't recall having seen, was lined with the tanned skin of moles. A boy of earlier times, part Cherokee and a great hunter, sat over mole runs and, upon hearing the working of feet digging beneath him, dug down, swooped up the critters, slaughtered them and cured and tanned the hides until he had enough to line his locker.

We played in the playroom in the winter, skinning the cat on the overhead waterpipes or building little tractors out of wooden matches, rubber bands, and empty thread spools. We clipped coupons out of *Colliers* and *Boys' Life* and sent them off for free samples of Ovaltine and Lifebuoy Soap. We used reams of paper trying to say something nice about Ivory soap and Palmolive soap only to see the prizes awarded to someone in Portland, Oregon, or East Orange, N. J.

We went to bed at nine o'clock and arose at six o'clock when a boy came around ringing a small brass bell. We went to breakfast when the bell rang again at six-thirty. Breakfast was usually oatmeal, never sweet enough, occasionally corn flakes or government surplus yellow grits. The dinner bell rang at noon. For dinner we had a lot of fresh vegetables in the summer, grown on our own farms, and canned vegetables and cornsticks in the winter. Supper was at five-thirty. On Tuesday, Thursday, and Saturday nights we had peanut butter, molasses, and bread. The other nights there were vegetables. On Sunday night we had a "hand-supper," a pickle relish sandwich, a peanut butter sandwich, and a wedge of pound cake without frosting.

In the dining room we sat at six wooden tables seating six each. We asked God to bless each meal. Miss Ballard and Mrs. Mellons took turns at breakfasts and dinners and at suppers sometimes called on one of the big boys. The blessing was always the same: "Oh Lord, bless this food to our bodies and us to Thy service." Before, during, and after the blessing children implemented strategies of speed and guile to ensure a successful meal. The first boy to the table claimed the privilege of first extra, the first cut of any thing left over after the original divisions. On Sundays the claim was to the choicest piece of chicken. "I speak for the drum stick" or "I speak for the pulley bone" was the way the girls said it. At the Chowan John and Cal learned to indicate their choices during the blessing by licking two fingers and marking their pieces or by plunging their forks into the breast or pulley bone.

Certain foods were proportioned by decree, not by choice. Collard greens, spinach, and turnip greens were ladled unto each plate and expected to be eaten. I failed to eat mine at dinner one day during the first week and Miss Ballard, who always checked to see if you ate your greens, took me by the arm, and on the way to the bathroom said "You must be sick." She gave me a tall glass of milk of magnesia to drink. I took a sip of the vile stuff, hunched my shoulders, leaned close over the sink and poured it out while pretending to drink. I ran the water to wash away the evidence. She was none the wiser. Thereafter, I never left greens on my plate nor did I eat them. At the last minute I scooped the soggy mess in hand and carried it out in my pocket.

Life at the orphanage settled into routines controlled by precisely timed bells, either the brass handbell in each cottage or the deep throated clapper in the church tower. A bell rang, we got up. A bell rang, we went to work or school. A bell rang, we came in for meals. A bell rang, we went to church, and so on, everything, interminably, a set time tuned to the vibrations of bells. Miss Ballard punished us if we didn't report when the bell rang by making us sit on the stairs inside while everyone else went out to play, or she made us stand in the corner on one foot.

John and Cal came to see me during visiting hour, from two

to three o'clock on Sunday. Otherwise we saw little of each other until vacation time. In February 1934, Miss Ballard decorated the Simmons dining room with balloons, streamers and bright table cloths and gave a birthday party of ice cream and cake. We birthday boys could invite our brothers and sisters and John and Cal were there.

With the coming of spring my conscious homesickness diminished and I joined happily in the traditional boys' games: scrub football, kick-the-can, marbles, hide, and also in those games with a distinct orphanage imprint; muffin and bringing-in.

Spring games began on the day we were allowed to go barefoot. Mr. Greer decreed that on the day a child brought him a blossom from the dogwood tree we could take off our shoes and go barefoot until fall. This usually occurred around April 15. With this singular event the energy surged and laughter and outright joy rang out as we ran through the tall grass in the valley.

Unencumbered by shoes, we Simmons boys established a point in the valley about forty yards away from the kitchen door and challenged each other to foot races to establish the fastest among us. The weather was cool and we were still wrapped in jackets and wearing knickers but we were loath to wait for winter to flee and were not about to put our shoes on again. For the race there was no limbering up. We stood crouched at the line and when ''on your mark, get set, go'' was called we were off, streaking through the cold dew to the point and back.

The foot race, like the fight, was a way of assigning informal positions in the pecking order. These positions were not binding, for we all fancied ourselves as stronger or faster than the other boy but he who was in that position one day might well trail into the cottage with a bloody nose on another. The foot races enabled me to edge up a notch or two in the pecking order for I was a faster runner than most of the smaller boys and faster than many of the larger ones.

On most days we finished work and play by cleaning up, splashing water on faces, hands and feet. We bathed and got clean underwear on Tuesday and Saturday. Helen Bell and other big girls helped with the bathing of smaller boys, but when we neared eight years old we preferred to do it ourselves. We scrubbed young skin with an abrasive bar of Lava soap until it was pink and shiny. Our ears were points examined to be certain that we bathed adequately.

We were allowed visits from family but Mama, Aunt Gus, and B. H. lived a long distance from Thomasville. They did come one Easter Sunday with Uncle Marion, in his large black Packard touring car with green shades. On our mother's side we were especially well endowed with uncles. Not so much by their numbers as by their qualities of behavior, which transformed them for us into figures of legend. Uncle Marion, or Mac as he was called, was a dark, quiet talker full of hidden strength. He possessed a way with women. As I first remember him he had gone off to California with my other uncles to seek their fortunes. He became a tree surgeon with a tree company and roamed the country. One year he would be in Maryland and the next in Oregon. Sometimes he came home for a visit driving a fine car and on other visits used his thumb. As a bachelor he had suffered almost continuous pursuit; but though slow in manner he was fleet of foot and had given the girls a long run. We always wondered if he were on the lam from the FBI. He sent reams of poetry to John to have it put to paper in the print shop.

On the day of the visit we rode in regal splendor leaving the orphanage grounds and touring Thomasville peering out through darkened windows. Looking for gas, we drove into a filling station which was closed. Upon leaving, Uncle Marion's car bumper caught the gas pump and jarred it so the gasoline seeped from its base. He got out, looked it over and decided it was of no moment to him and drove off. We were never clear about the outcome but Aunt Gus kidded him years later about getting caught on the way home by the State Patrol.

In June we went on vacation for a week. Mama and Aunt Gus sent money for train tickets and a date was set for us to go to Black Mountain. The suspense before vacation was unbearable. Miss Ballard sent my clothes over to the Chowan to be packed in the suitcase with John and Cal's and on the fateful day Mr. Millsap, the mailman, drove us to the depot to board the Asheville train.

John was always in charge. We changed trains either at Salisbury or Barber Junction or both and I was always badgering John and Cal to buy me something to eat in the depot cafe. It was a long day's trip but once we had made the final switch and were safely aboard the Asheville train we had no worry of being hungry. One conductor, Mr. John Jones, was an old orphanage boy and he always sensed when orphanage children were on his train. He treated us royally, pushed seat backs to create a large seat so that he could sit with us and point out Andrew's geyser at Old Fort and other interesting things as we rode in and out of tunnels on the upward grade to Black Mountain. He bought us ham sandwiches with white bread and chocolate milk from vendors who walked the aisles. In Black Mountain Hub Morehead always met us at the station and took us home for a joyous reunion with Mama, Aunt Gus, and B. H.

Our week at home passed too quickly and after each return we felt again the homesickness and loneliness but gradually the periods became shorter and shorter as we became more involved in orphanage life.

The remainder of the summer was spent in playing: at the swimming pool, in the valley, on the playground. I began forming friendships with other boys, Ralph Hill, Clarence Green, Donald Harrelson, Paul Smith.

Most of our games were competitive and physical and pitted us against one another. Some boys were less strong and came under Miss Ballard's protection as her pets. Reece Gardner was a small, thin, red-haired boy who always had severely chapped lips. Miss Ballard watched over him in particular. Being a matron's pet invited derision, and they were continually picked on by the other boys.

The worst fate that could befall an orphanage boy was to be considered a sissy. We all cried from loneliness or homesickness during our first few months and this was tolerated. But prolonged weepiness earned a boy the title of cry baby. The cry baby was not the same as being a sissy, a form of unmanliness. I avoided being designated as either cry baby or sissy, but continued to have occasional crying spells until one day Fat Green found me crying in the furnace room where he had come to clean out the clinkers and to fill the stoker with coal. He asked me what the matter was and then put his arms around my shoulder. "Don't be sad," he said. "Sometimes it's tough but it's not all bad here." I don't recall crying any more after that.

Mrs. Mellons made life happier for us. She was a widow with children of her own in Tennessee. She was affectionate, warm-hearted, and had the patience and sympathy to listen to our troubles. During winter Saturdays we were forced outdoors to play in cold weather clad in short pants, shirts and thin jackets. Our hands were always raw and chapped so deep they looked as though they had been cut. We shivered, shook, and pressed close into the corners of chimneys to keep warm. The earth there always smelled strongly of urine. We knocked on the kitchen door and gratefully entered the warm room with its good smells of sheets of gingerbread. We persuaded Mrs. Mellons that a tiny piece would not spoil our lunch and we would not let Miss Ballard know. After Mrs. Mellons retired she continued to communicate by mail with dozens of boys who loved her.

We attended church three times a week, Sunday morning and evening, and Wednesday evening prayer meeting. The Greek style auditorium had large columns, wide steps and big doors. It gave a sense of security to enter it as a place of worship. Each cottage had its appointed seating section. We Simmons boys sat up in the balcony. Service began with the singing of a grand hymn or two. When the refrain called for us to "March to Zion," to a man we were prepared to step out. A darker boyish side showed up in church when we irreverently parodied the grand and serious words of "At the Cross" into a jingle: "At the Cross, at the cross where I first saw the light, and the money in my pocket rolled away. It was there by gosh and now it's gone and I am sad all the day." For such irreverence and for falling asleep or talking, Miss Ballard thumped heads with bony fingers and sent guilty parties to bed on Sunday afternoons.

Sunday after Sunday Mr. Neilson, our pastor, preached about Jesus — how He lived and how we should try to live as He did. As we listened we faced a giant oil painting hanging above the pastor's head. In the picture Jesus sat at a watering trough among the sheep and shepherds with one child on his lap and with a hand on the head of another. The painting was a gift from the architect who had designed the auditorium; a gift for the children, painted by the giver. Week after week we looked at Jesus and the children and listened to Mr. Neilson and slowly we began to absorb the immanence of Jesus. Stripped of specifics, the orphanage was Jesus. My sense of belonging became real. I was an orphanage boy. Jesus loved orphans. Jesus loved me.

The orphanage became the place of my roots. I absorbed the flavor of its sounds, smells, and people and when things were right in all its places, I was no longer sad. The orphanage became vital to me. There was no alienation and when away on vacation, I contemplated my return. By my first September, when school started I was well into becoming an orphanage boy. Those who had jeered and fought me earlier were now my friends.

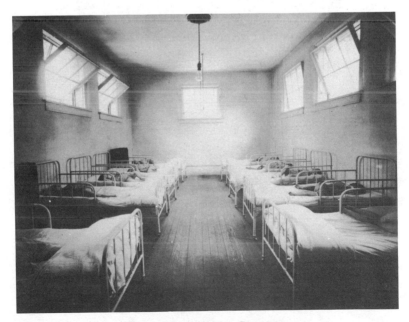

Dormitory at the Simmons

Miss Ballard, Mrs. Mellons and their boys.

6

School

In September school loomed and to prepare me I was hustled off to the infirmary to have my tonsils out, a prophylactic ritual to which all orphanage boys and girls were subjected. I began school on Monday, 17 September 1934, in a two-room brick building with first and second grades at ground level and music practice in the basement. The first grade room was packed with tables of sand, colored paper, rolls and shapes of clay, and toys such as I'd never seen before, We began with a class of about thirty, but the number in the class changed yearly as some pupils scored high on the Metropolitan Achievement Tests and skipped a grade. Others were held back a grade for scoring low. My time in the first and second grades was a brief but cozy anarchy. In that short period I played and wept, broke things, fell asleep, buttered up the teacher, discovered what I could get by with, and exhaled my last guiltless days.

John and Cal started school in the regular school building, a "U" shaped building adjoined to the church. The church served as chapel for school events. The rooms of grades three, four, and five faced those of six, seven, and eight, opening across a wide, continuous, railed porch onto an inner courtyard. There we played during recess and lined up to march into the classrooms. Our rooms had oily, creaking floors, swept daily with dusteen, high, wide windows, blackboards covering the entire wall behind the teacher's desk, naked-light bulbs, high ceilings, and wooden desks carved with the initials of the occupants of the past fifty years.

John was in fifth grade and Cal in third. We had scarcely begun before John's name began appearing on the first honor roll. Cal and I moved at a more normal pace, content to serve out our time, to slop around, and idle away our hours in spite of our teachers' pleadings. So we followed after, living in John's shadow, occasionally hitting a streak of ambition that proved our stuff; we could also make the honor roll.

Suddenly, almost to my dismay, I found that I could count up to a hundred, write my name in both large and small letters, subtract certain numbers from each other, read, tie my shoes, and tell time. Child no longer, I was moved up — third grade was ready for me.

I found there a world both adult and tough, with long desks and inkwells, strange maps on the walls, big boys, pretty girls, scratching pens and pencils, groans of labor and sharp and sudden retribution. Gone forever were the childish excuses, the sanctuary of my mediocrity. Now I was more alone and unprotected, faced by a struggle which required new techniques, where one became more resourceful in choosing friends and making pacts.

Miss Warner, my third grade teacher, was short with bobbed hair and rimless glasses. She indoctrinated us to the wonders of life among the bullfrogs by hiking us down the farm road to the swamp. Beneath the green slime on placid water we seined for tadpoles, put them in a glass jar and took them to the classroom where we housed them in a sustaining environment. We watched them metamorphose into full-bodied frogs as they grew legs and dropped tails.

Orphans with inadequate brain power were not taken into the orphanage but those who were simply too lazy, too sassy, or too dirty to toe the mark soon recognized their match. Miss Hayes in the fourth and Miss Beavers in the sixth were mild and amiable on the outside but did not brook interference in their march to make scholars of us all.

Miss Johnson in the fifth was responsible for many a good reflex. Red hair coiled at the nape of her neck, she whacked the desk each morning with a ruler, roved the class looking for boys with an evil nature or occult cunning and when faced with an infraction dealt with it straightway. She coiled, uncoiled and sprang, catching the perpetrator by the hand. Extending it to the limit she whacked with the ruler straight edge until the punishment neutered the crime. Criminal girls were punished similarly but more gently. They consoled themselves by hugging the insulted hand under the opposite arm.

Grave offenses were referred to Coach Kearns, who was a virtuoso with a wooden paddle, a relic of fraternity hazing at Furman. He kept the tool hanging by a leather thong on his office wall. Operational routine was always the same, and every boy knew it as intimately as he knew the the rules of marbles or football. The condemned would be beckoned to the place of execution in his office and at the words "get ready" from the coach he would hold up his hands, and bend over until his fingers grazed his ankles. The punitive swooshes would follow, sometimes two, three or even four, but more often only one. It was unthinkable for the condemned to make an outcry, but he was allowed and even expected to massage his gluteus maximus vigorously as he pranced back to the classroom.

The coach showed very little moral indignation when he carried on such exercises and victims did not denounce the punishments as unjust, undoubtably convinced that they were sound in law and equity, and necessary to peace and civilization. The practice was stopped when George Bailey took umbrage and reported to Mr. Greer. He called a halt, which suited coach Kearns because he always took much more visible delight in rewards than in punishments anyhow.

Cal was office boy for Mr. Skaggs, the principal, and a few times he was sent to him for punishment. Mr. Skaggs listened to his confession, sat him down at a desk with a book or pencil and paper, and when time enough had passed sent him back to the teacher. Mr. Skaggs introduced the game of golf on the orphanage by using a pasture as a driving range. Cal helped him fashion a couple of holes for his short game and on Saturdays, while he practiced, shagged balls for him. Cal protected Mr. Skagg's mini course as well as he could, but golf was a strange and unfamiliar pastime and the barn boys were forever filling the holes with cow manure. Soon Mr. Skaggs took his game to a nearby golf course and both John and Cal caddied for him.

School seemed to me then to be designed simply to keep us out of the air and from following normal pursuits of the fields. Miss Johnson's science of dates and sums kept us locked in our stocks, our backs bent, our minds tuned to the woods and creek. I was reading book after book of adventure, of life among the Indians, or life at sea, and I gazed through the windows as the spring air infected my day-dreaming with unbelievable exploits of heroism as I rescued damsel after damsel from certain destruction. We all smelt the fields and were tormented by the cries of killdeers down near the barns. Every out-of-door sound that came drifting in was a sharp nudge in the solar plexus. The creaking of wagons going past the school, harness jingle, chattering mowing machines, truckloads of boys on their way to the fields, all tugged and pulled at our active wishes till we could have done Miss Johnson in, given a chance.

And indeed there came the inevitable day when rebellion broke out and a hero, unlikely as he was, emerged. Frank Bailey told me about him. He should have been given a medal for his exploits. At least from that day, his exploit was honored, though he received little support at the time.

Roy Allaberg it was. He was a heavy, over-grown boy, thick-legged, red-fisted, bursting with flesh, designed for the great outdoors. He was nearly thirteen then and physically out of scale — at least so far as the fifth grade was concerned. The sight of him squeezed into his tiny desk was worse than having Duke, our Holstein bull, in basketball shorts. Roy wasn't much of a scholar; he groaned as he worked, or hacked at his desk with a pocketknife. Miss Johnson forced him to read out loud; or asked him sudden, unintelligible questions which made him flush and stumble.

Roy preferred to sit and pitch wadded paper balls at the wastebasket. He missed often and retrieved his missed shots by crawling across the floor on hands and knees, eyes flashing and big head switching back and forth so that he could look up girls' dresses.

The day came; a day of shimmering spring, with the great oaks outside burst out in a new leafy coat. Miss Johnson had had all she could take of Roy, and he was at his sourest. Frank didn't quite know what the matter was that made the difference, but suddenly Roy was expelled. She told him to "get out" in angry tones as her face suffused with a crimson glow. Frank giggled and was sent to join him. The rest of the class laid down their pencils and watched silently. Outside, Roy looked at Frank and said, "Come on, Frank. Let's go the woods."

For such an infraction terrible retribution was expected and it happened. Soon Roy mysteriously disappeared, destination unknown to us. Frank Bailey was held back by Miss Johnson that year, to join Miss Nell Joyner's class, but made up the lost time by being jumped to Miss Beaver's sixth grade when his achievement test showed that he was doing work good enough for the second month, eighth grade.

But most of us never rebelled. We left Miss Johnson and passed to Miss Beaver, Miss Olney, Miss Quattlebaum, and others. We passed from *The Primer, The Little Red Hen, The Gingerbread Boy, The Old Woman and The Pig, Chicken Little, Three Billy Goats Gruff, Little Spider's First Web* to *The Graded Classics, The Japanese Twins, The Open Door, The World's Wonders*. The reins of authority of our teachers were loose but strong, and each year after the first hilarity of the opening of school passed we settled down and accepted our teacher's proper authority.

In 1934, the psychologists were convinced that tales of gore, violence, and death such as *Little Red Riding Hood, Blackbeard,* and *Jack and the Beanstalk* would cause young impressionable minds to become fixated on evil or to be subject to psychoses later in life. In the lower grades these were standard fare, and we listened as Miss White told the tale of the young girl in the red cape taking butter to her grandmother. We shuddered when the deceptive and vicious wolf stalked into the scene and gobbled up grandma and was about to do the same for Little Red Riding Hood. We cheered when a convenient woodchopper rushed up in the nick of time and saved her. We chanted "Fee fie foe fum, I smell the blood of an Englishman; be he alive or be he dead, I'll grind his bones to make my bread." We learned to read and the tales were of witches, cruel step-mothers, kidnappers and evil encounters. We were hardier plants than the psychologists gave us credit for being.

We learned nothing abstract or tenuous in our school — just simple patterns of facts and letters, tricks of calculation that would help us make change, measure for a building, or write out a bill. Through the dead hours of the morning, through the long afternoons, we chanted away at our tables and learned spelling words. Along the way we were receiving aphoristic treasures from the teacher: an ounce of prevention is worth a pound of cure, a merry heart doeth good like a medicine. Each word was like a lesson: Deny, do not deny your fault. The thief denies his guilt. Charles denied that he whispered. We copied sentences until we knew their truths by heart: Life is but a means to an end; bleak blows the blast; least said is soonest mended; be of good cheer. When we came to, "Her locks are like a golden fleece," followed by "Drink, pretty creature, drink," I shyly looked over at the locks of Mary Frances Kirk, the prettiest girl in the third grade. The outrageous and wonderful thoughts I had at nine years old were brought to a crash with: "Pleasure oft is the lure to sin," followed by "The guilty soul dreads death," and "A good name needs no scouring."

In the spring the Bird Woman visited each class and captivated us with lifelike creations of common birds with colored chalk. Field glasses dangling, she took us to the woods and taught us to imitate the killdeer and the titmouse. These same woods beckoned to us on Saturdays and Sundays, and in them and Hamby Creek we caught snakes, frogs, lizards, and flying squirrels, but we loved her so much that the birds were safe from the rocks of our slingshots.

We caught animals in the woods and tried to domesticate them to the ways of school. But, sometimes animals ran loose and teachers lost tolerance amid general disruption as everyone tried to corner a flying squirrel or green snake. Miss Quattlebaum stopped music class in the middle of ''My Bonnie Lies Over the Ocean,'' to ask about a particular bass sound, and Judy Woods confessed that it was his frog trying to join the music lesson.

We began school at 7:10 a.m. and continued until 5:00 p.m. but were divided into two groups — one-half attended the morning session and one-half the afternoon. While one group was at school the other was at work. At noon we gathered for lunch and afterwards switched, with the workers becoming scholars and the scholars workers. At night we had a two-hour study hall with our matron in attendance. Recess was a short but intense break in the middle of a four-hour school day. We charged outdoors, releasing our steamed-up cries and descended into a dark, dirty, wet bathroom with three commodes and one urinal expected to meet the needs of ninety boys in fifteen minutes, and allow time to shoot a few marbles, punch somebody's head, or cluster round like bees for a few minutes of football. It wasn't much, fifteen minutes or so, but we hated it when we had to give it up as punishment.

Our school reeked of steaming life: boys came in their brogans, fresh from the cow barn, chicken lot, pig pen; bare feet in due season, overalls, and denim shirts. The girls came in clean dresses, some with sashes, polished slippers, clean smelling hair, some clasped with bows, and carrying neatly arranged books.

The boy in love was easily spotted. He was clean and his hair pasted down with good smelling goo.

There was the smell of sweat, blue ink, white chalk, and shavings from the pencil sharpeners. Each classroom had its own voice and passersby could hear us reciting; ''twelve inches make a foot, three feet make a yard, nine plus seven is sixteen''. We absorbed facts and figures as primal truths declared by some ultimate power. We asked few questions; we didn't hear what we said;

yet neither did we ever forget it.

From country bred boys and girls Mr. and Mrs. Lord, our music directors, gradually accumulated a sizable number interested in blowing horns, beating drums, singing in glee clubs, quartets, or trios. After the Lords had identified those with talent true and minds teachable we soon heard strains of Sousa and America The Beautiful coming from the music room.

Mr. Lord anguished over my french horn playing but finally decided in the interest of the band as a whole that music was not my line of ability and asked that I hand in my instrument. John tried for the cornet but only got silent wind from it. In music we were cut from the same cloth. Cal became a drummer, a position that required only deft hands and a foot that could keep time as Mr. Lord looked his way or indicated, with the baton, that he should begin or desist.

Soon Sousa had us. We won music awards competing with other bands, built a bandstand for out-of-doors concerts, had band music during chapel, and followed marching forms resplendent in red and white uniforms with Sam Brown belts and peaked caps. The robust, muscular, airy wildness of Sousa's music had us. It took us over, and we strutted to blue spangling heaven and heard poetry rhymed on the wind.

Of course we had to have a bandstand. It became a showpiece, perched on the hill behind the library. It was an octagonal structure thirty by thirty, with a high pointed roof, a wooden floor and a railing. There, on fair special evenings we sat on the hill and listened as the music makers made merry and at dark we walked home in a warm glow.

Most of the boys and girls in the band were quite ordinary with the brass horns and reeds, but a few stood out as born with musical talent hitherto undiscovered. Milton Bliss and Randolph Robbins on clarinet and John Brinegar on cornet entertained us with an evening of music just prior to their graduation from high school. They performed a sophisticated program in song or on their horns. "You'll Remember Me" from Bohemian Girl was followed by "La Marsiellaise," "Requiem," "The Waterfall," "Legende," "Sing Ho! for the Rolling Sea," "Toreador Song,"

"Andante," "Polanaise," "Cornfield Melodies", and "Shoo Fly Don't Bother Me."

Milton had come to the orphanage when he was ten years old. His early days there were filled with loneliness and homesickness for his mother, even though while with her he had no clean bed sheets, vegetables, milk, eggs, and clean clothes as he now had.

On weekends he wandered alone down the road to the creek, singing at the top of his voice, songs that he made up as he walked. It was a way of relieving his sadness. His only remembrance of music was vivid; a radio playing a classical recording by a symphonic orchestra. At the time, it struck him as the most beautiful thing he had ever experienced. He wept.

Milton lived at the Durham Cottage with Grady Morrison and other boys. He and Grady were sitting in the study reading one evening and Grady got up to go out. "See you later," he said.

"Where you going?"

"To band practice."

"Can I come," Milton asked.

"Nope, you don't play a horn."

"I can learn."

"Oh, okay, come on."

Milton sat listening and watching as the others oiled the valves of their horns and squeaked their way through practice amidst the distinctive metal and oil smell that comes from brass and reed instruments. He thought the music was beautiful and fidgeted through each practice itching to get his fingers on a horn.

"Don't you have an instrument I can play?" he asked Mr. Lord.

"Only an old clarinet, not a good one."

"I'll take it," Milton said.

One thing followed another, the piano followed the clarinet, and voice training was next. Mr. and Mrs. Lord were a remarkably talented couple who captured our attention with their sparkle, wit, and enthusiasm and brought to the surface the tiniest shred of talent in hundreds of boys and girls.

Those of us who strove to be musicians and failed, looked

69

to our other teachers to show us how to drill through mud and water for oil, how to sift through silt for the gold, and to chip and hack through stones for the diamonds within. In the seventh grade I inhaled deeply and began:

Breathes there a man, with soul so dead, Who never to himself hath said, This is my own, my native land...

Miss Holder sat waiting for the end, and with suitable gestures I came, at length, to the finale: "If such there breathe, living shall forfeit fair renown/and doubly dying shall go down/to the vile dust from which he sprung,/unwept, unhonored and unsung." We all recited away quite happily, and much of what we learned remains a pleasant resource even now.

We began our foray into the art of declamation with Miss Hayes in the fourth grade, and we learned such sonerous verses by the yard. At the farm I never saw Mr. Paul that I did not recall the lines from "The Village Blacksmith."

Under a spreading chestnut tree
    The Village smithy stands,
The smith a mighty man is he,
    With large and sinewy hands;
And the muscles of his brawny arms
    Are strong as iron bands.

He goes on Sunday to the church,
    And sits among his boys;
He hears the parson pray and preach;
    He hears his daughter's voice,
Singing in the Village choir,
    And it makes his heart rejoice.

Toiling, — rejoicing, — and sorrowing,
    Onward through life he goes;
Each morning sees some task begin,
    Each evening sees it close;
Something attempted, something done,
    Has earned a night's repose.

Thanks, thanks to thee, my working friend,
  For the lesson thou hast taught!
Thus at the flaming forge of life
  Our fortunes must be wrought;
Thus on its sounding anvil shaped
  Each burning deed and thought.

We especially liked the more morbid poems dealing with death and untimely demise. We were prepared to go with Bryant:

...not, like the quarry-slave at
  night,
Scourged to his dungeon, but
  sustained and soothed,
By an unfaltering trust, approach
  Thy grave
Like one who wraps the drapery
  of his couch
About him and lies down to
  pleasant dreams.

We learned much prose and memorized a sizable number of poems, and a good deal of Shakespeare. In doing so, we partook of an older tradition represented by the McGuffey Readers. Our language and history books contained dozens of great set pieces from America's past — such things as The Declaration of Independence, Washington's Farewell Address, Patrick Henry's "Give me Liberty or Give me Death," and the Gettysburg Address.

These pieces gave us contact with the great figures and the great epochs of the past. Reciting before the class, we experienced vicariously the heroic episodes, and become ourselves Horatius at the bridge, Mark Anthony orating over the bier of his fallen chief, Henry V at Agincourt, Patrick Henry defying tyranny. Words thus committed to memory echoed in the inner consciousness. They constituted dramatic embodiment of those old-fashioned oddities — moral values.

At the same time, in biology, we were memorizing our body

parts from a diagram on the blackboard. We were totally immersed in the study. The relationship between the diagram and our own selves got a workout the morning Robert Belch reported to Miss Rucker, at the infirmary, holding his side in mortal agony. Miss Rucker rushed to him and asked what was the matter. "Don't know exactly, Miss Rucker," groaned Robert, "but it feels like my ovaries are about to bust wide open!"

Some of us spent a good bit of our youth in prolonged warfare against academic proprieties. It was not the resistance of our precocious and imaginative minds against dull routine. It was the resistance of vague and lazy minds to imaginative routines. Rather than give us up as "a pretty blank page," our teachers were more likely to dedicate themselves to helping us find ourselves; to resetting our compass in a straight direction. Franklin Bailey's downward slide was stopped by Miss Council.

Frank had been caught selling stolen chickens for twenty-five cents each to cotton mill workers who lived at Amazon Hill. He was put on punishment washing dishes and on Saturday afternoon, was remanded to the creek bank where he cut brush alongside other members of the junior chain gang. He was shamed and humiliated by the association with other boys on punishment and by the name, the junior chain gang. He ran away. His grandfather, in Davie County, brought him back. Miss Council sent for him. "Now, Franklin," she said, "you're a better boy than that. You're capable. You need to take the punishment." Frank decided he had started a run at "Fool's Hill," and took his punishment. He was determined to not run away again and to finish school, and he did.

Miss Council was tall, thin as a reed, and had white hair. She was our librarian and moved among the books in a whisper advising boys and girls what to read to build our minds. She taught penmanship and encouraged each of us to a more graceful style. She had great discernment into the difference between what we wanted to read and what we should read. Her mind was sharp and analytical.

Each summer we had reading contests and handwork projects. Our names were listed on a large board with a border of book jackets. We earned four points for each book of non-fiction and two points for each book of fiction and in September, during the first chapel of the new school year, prizes were awarded. In 1937-38 Carrie Frances Carden read fifty books from June 1 to September 1. Miss Olive awarded her a book of poems *It Can Be Done*. Ronnie Baldwin won in the contest for the best books read and reported on during the month of August. The winning list was *Jane Eyre, Pilgrim's Progress, Les Miserables* and *King Lear*. Miss Sallie gave her a copy of *Pilgrim's Progress* as a prize.

We read Scott, Dickens, Jack London's *The Cruise of the Dazzler*, Joseph Altsheler's *The Young Trailers, Careers of Danger and Daring, Boys Useful Pastimes, Ten Nights in a Bar Room and What I Saw There*. We read books required for parallel reading from a list approved by Miss Olive, our English teacher. Some of us were a year ahead. We supplemented our farm and dairy education with peeks at the bared breasts of dark skinned African natives in *The National Geographic*. We learned about each other and about behavior that was beyond our imagination by reading *The Anatomy of Personality, Do Adolescents Need Parents?, Guiding Human Misfits,* and *The Sex Criminal*.

The mere mention of a book in a sermon or address sent us to the library by the score to find it. The dramatization of a novel into a movie made it impossible to fill the demand. Often Miss Council designed treasure hunts or other games to entice us to read more. We did not always read what she advised, but she was quick to replace objectionable books as she checked our choices at the checkout desk.

One of the main themes of my younger days at the orphanage was the untiring warfare with Mr. Richardson on the farm, Mr. Amos at the dairy, and Miss Hester at the Mother's Cottage, who objected to my general shiftlessness, which, to them, was expressed in the constant reading of books of dubious merit and morals. I, showing the same patient guile that I employed to evade schoolwork, read on the vegetable wagon, in the milkcooling room, by flashlight in bed, in the furnace room, huddled in a corner of the study, or wherever I could find a brief refuge. The war over my reading continued until I graduated.

First honor roll was a grade of 93 or more, perfect attendance, and perfect conduct. John made it almost every month and in the ninth grade won an award for the highest grades in the Thomasville schools. His prize was a ten dollar pen and pencil set. Cal followed, doing well but falling short of John's mark. My progress was erratic; honor roll one month, mediocrity the next. It depended on how much window gazing and day dreaming I did.

In our senior year the boys of my class, to a man, signed up for Home Economics under Miss Edwards, a prim lady who insisted that orphanage boys reform their habits of hunching over their plates at meals, as though someone was going to make off with the food. Near the end of the year, with the help of the girls in the class, we gave a breakfast for all the teachers. The main course was omelet, the only dish we learned to cook during the year. Leonard Evans and I greeted our guests, Harry Crapps served plates, and Bob Yarborough and Steven Batts were the cooks. During the next chapel period Audrey Bowman delivered a declaration on: "How to Cook a Husband."

So our schoolwork was done. We entered the door marked "infants and children," moved gradually through each stop, and were then handed back to the world. Near the end our teachers began to ask our advice about the senior play and graduation, and to spoil us as though we were dying. There was no more to be done, no more to be learned. We began to look round the schoolroom with nostalgia and impatience. During recess we walked about gravely, patronizing the younger creatures. No longer the trembling, white-faced battles, the flights, the buttering-up of bullies, just a punch here and there to show our authority, then a sober stroll with our peers.

We moved through the festivities of class day, practiced and performed the likes of the "Absent Minded Professor," and "Let Polly Fix It," to an audience of over 1,000, and on to the day of receiving our diplomas and Bibles.

Our school taught subjects that today would be called a traditional curriculum: the old math (the kind one actually uses in life), spelling as old as Websters, geography full of capitals, and history full of heroes and patriotism. We memorized, deriving

74

much benefit-spiritual, moral, rhetorical-in getting those splendid phrases and concepts in our growing minds and psyches.

Years later, on the first day of internship, after I received my M.D. degree, my first patient was Miss Bost, my sociology teacher. She refused an examination by me. I was so relieved. She had thrown a book at me in the ninth grade to wake me up, and I guess she was amazed that here I was all fresh and educated...and awake.

Miss Council in her library.

Commercial class.

The Faculty — 1937
Back row: Mr. Lord, Mr. Skaggs, Mr. McCulloch, Mr. Kearns.
Middle row: Mrs. McColloch, Miss Olney, Nell Joyner,
Margaret Joyner, Miss Hayes, Miss Council, Miss Beavers.
Front row: Mrs. Lord, Miss Johnson, Miss Booth, Miss Olive,
Miss Stroupe, Miss Warner.

Our band. Cal is at the right end of the last row with his snare
drum.

7

Duty

There was work aplenty on the orphanage. My first taste came when I was assigned my duty after two days into life at the Simmons Cottage. Towering above me Miss Ballard's lean form peered through thick glasses, handed me a short handle brush and dustpan and with a long skinny finger pointed to two stairs of 16 steps each. "This is your duty," she said, "Brush those twice daily, after breakfast and after supper." Duty was that simple, nothing to argue over, a mandate, life's whole purpose, just do it. And I did, for a year, day after day. By that time I had grown a little and had made friends with Clarence Green and Ralph Hill and early in the morning of the first Monday in September we sat on tree roots or milled around with a hundred other boys before the porch of a small shack known as the farm office. We were there to learn our fate, our duty for the next five months.

This assemblage, in front of the farm office on the first Mondays of September and January, was a special ritual, known as change of duty day. The rotund figure of Mr. McKoin stood on the porch and spat tobacco juice, and boy's names, and the expression "John Brown" until each boy had answered "Here," and been given a duty. We were assigned to the farm, dairy, print shop, shoe shop, or as house or kitchen boy in a cottage, or as an office boy. We little boys went from job to job every change of duty day, but at age twelve were assigned to the farm, dairy, or print shop to learn a trade.

Clarence, Ralph, and I were assigned to the farm under the direction of Mr. Paul Edinger. Mr. Paul had the farm crew creating additional crop land by clearing a patch of woods at the edge of Rose's field. Each morning he warmed his hands at the iron stove and looked us over. He pointed to Ralph Pounders, Carl Watson, Mike Ray, and Marvin Miller, all big boys and each with his own team, tractor, or truck. He assigned a dozen or more of us small boys as helpers, "You, you, and you are to go clear new ground."

We pulled bushaxs, mattocks, and hoes from tool bins and waited in line to sharpen edges on a rumbling grinding wheel that spewed orange sparks that pitted and burned bare legs.

Clearing new ground in winter without gloves was miserable work. We stuffed raw, chapped hands in shallow pockets of short pants and pulled thin jackets over our middles to keep out the frigid air. We hugged the shadows of the tool room, kept from getting close by the big boys sitting around on wooden crates. They hated to give up even the tiniest bit of warmth from the glowing fire box. We waited until the last possible moment and then dashed out and sprinted to catch the wagon or truck to the new ground. We preferred to sit and talk, roast corn on the hot stove top, smell the wood smoke, and watch spit sizzle against the firey belly. We were permitted to do that only when the snow or rain was too fierce for us. Otherwise we got what heat we could and moved out.

We piled in wagons with our weapons and like an army rode forth to conquer. Mules were hitched to drag pans and were steered and cajoled to tear the earth and make level the high places. They strained and unearthed great rocks that were rolled to the edges. Mr. Paul did not allow boys to beat animals, but we did encourage them to the limit. Clarence, Ralph, and I hacked at roots and stumps, carried limbs and threw them on a huge bonfire, or carried water for the crew. We cut down saplings, leaving the larger trees to be chopped by the big boys. We returned home at the end of the day, dirty, tired, and hungry. I worked at clearing new ground and at other farm work for two years and then, for the time, my farm life ended; I became Miss Sallie's office boy.

Miss Sallie was secretary to Mr. Greer. She was mountain-bred, auburn-haired, widely traveled, and a saver. Nothing was willingly discarded. She kept neat stacks of magazines for a while and then sent them to the library. She sent office boys to scout trash cans of discarded mail for stamps to tear off. She tolerated no overalls or brogans. It was white shirts and scrubbed skin. We ran errands, carried the newspaper to each cottage and sat quietly awaiting her bidding. Sometimes we rode to town with her in her shiny black Oldsmobile.

I hated working indoors and Miss Sallie's outside work was even worse. She had a magical touch with flowers. She could snatch a dry root from a field or hedge-row, dab it into her garden, give it a shake and almost immediately it flowered. She could probably have grown roses from a stick or chair leg, so remarkable was her gift.

A triangular garden near the church was her monument and she controlled it closely, but she hated to weed. During her seventy-three years at the orphanage she must have supervised the pulling of at least a million weeds. We office boys were indoctrinated to the trowel, shears, hoe, shovel, and a ball of twine. We were drafted to weed out the wiregrass from the center-point of forget-me-nots or hollyhocks but beyond wiregrass could not make out the difference between weeds and non-weeds. So, it was a never-ending horticultural instructional course to distinguish between verminous and non-verminous growth.

I tackled the job with tools at hand, disliking it as much as I would have were I a convict on the chain gang on a public road. Weeding Miss Sallie's flower beds was part of the day to day assignment in that duty. It was not a punishment for grave offenses such as stealing from her candy jar, climbing in the wisteria over the Mother's building, or telling lies in a gross and obvious manner, but I hated it none the less.

I quickly tired of the work and grew quarrelsome. One day, while Miss Sallie was at a Woman's Club meeting, I got into a fight with David Cheek, the other office boy. It was over which one was going to empty the trash can. After rolling on the grass long enough to dirty white shirts, I caught David in a vise of iron. "Give up?" I asked.

"Yeah," he answered.

I believed him and let him up. He was mad. He whirled into me, arms and legs flailing. He kicked as hard as Old Red, one of our mules. An elbow caught me in the nose and blood gushed, onto shirt, onto pants, onto pride. I stood with glazed eyes and bloody face and begged for a truce so that we could clean up before Miss Sallie returned. She came too soon and looked us over, swollen faces, bloody rags, skinned knees and elbows but gave no word of condemnation. Only disdain. The look was punishment and we cowed and cringed for days.

I was forever scheming for a way out of Miss Sallie's employ. In January 1938, the excitement of a change of duty day gave me courage and I stood before Mr. McKoin, and when he called my name and asked if Miss Sallie wanted me again, I lied and said no. He assigned me to the farm again.

My joy was short-lived. After chapel service Miss Sallie crooked her finger and beckoned me to her. "Let's go to work," she said.

"I don't work for you anymore."

"Is that so?"

It was not so. She had Mr. McKoin change my duty and I ran errands, carried papers, tore stamps from old envelopes, and weeded flower beds for another year. Later, when Miss Sallie was in her nineties and reflected on her office boys, she mentioned those who were memorable, Cleve Wilkie, Graham Proctor and others, but never Ted Chandler.

In the summer of 1939, I was assigned to the farm as helper to Charlie Godwin. He drove a team of mules, Maud and Sally, and each day we began with the ritual of brushing and curry-combing until dust and sweat were flicked away and coats shone.

We grew wheat, barley, oats, and corn for grinding into feed for our cows, horses, pigs, and chickens. In 1939, Mr. McKoin's feed list for the year included: wheat — 1,000 bushels, corn — 3,950 bushels, oats — 1,760 bushels, barley — 2,400 bushels, cotton seed meal — 15 1/2 tons, wheat bran — 18 tons, fish and meat meal — 12 tons, bone meal — 5 1/2 tons, hay — 350 tons, ensilage — 350 tons, and linseed meal — 8 1/2 tons. All this for 100 hogs, averaging 300 pounds apiece, 150 head of cattle, 2,500 chickens, and 18 horses and mules.

Threshing season began on June 13 in 1939; the grain had yellowed, the sun was high and we were ready. We got ready by following the binder through field after field as it cut and tied grain into bundles; leaving sharp stubble to gouge shoeless feet. We stacked the bundles into shocks, and capped each by bending two bundles across the top to ward off rain.

Mr. Paul went to town and on a certain street corner walked among a crowd of jobless men and picked eight. They climbed aboard his truck and joined 15-20 large boys and a like number of small ones. All the street workers were black and we were white but Mr. Paul knew the mix worked well. He had regular supervising adult black men working in the chain of command: Robert Payne, Ernest Pringle, Uncle Tom Thompson, and Tom Klause.

The Long Field was the first for threshing. Charlie and I drove our wagon with its wide hay frame from stack to stack and boys with pitchforks tossed bundle after bundle aboard until we were loaded. With great expectation and excitement we watched as in the distance Mr. Coltrane came closer, down the farm road, across Hamby's Creek, and around the curve, pulling his marvelous giant contraption of wheels, pulleys, belts, and long metal tubes behind a high-stepping team.

He moved the thresher with confidence and positioned it in a flat spot cranking levers and adjusting blocks of wood until it was true and level to his eye's measure. We stood about, leaned on pitchforks, sat high on the wagonload of bundles of grain, or laughed on truck beds listening to man and boy talk as he made the final adjustment. Our hearts beat strong and fast when the tractor was started. Mr. Coltrane threw a lever and a long black belt moved and in turn brought to life the visible and invisible wheels and other mysteries housed in the bowels of the machine.

When all was ready our team pulled the wagon alongside the loading platform and I cut the twine binding each bundle before Charlie threw the bundles onto the platform with a pitchfork. On the platform another boy forked the bundles into the thresher and it groaned and chattered and spat out a continuous stream of grain kernels midst a cloud of chafing dust that contained atrocious barbs that relentlessly clung in our throats, causing us to cough in unyielding spasms.

At the end of a long metal pipe the grain spilled forth, fell through two sieves into a half-bushel bucket. Two boys poured the filled buckets into burlap bags. A bag of wheat or rye contained two bushels and weighed 120 pounds. Two bushels of barley weighed 96 pounds, and oats 64 pounds.

The thresher also spat out a steady stream of straw into the hopper of a baler and a boy sat on an iron seat poking two baling wires at proper intervals into the compressed straw as it moved along. Another worker, on the other side, pulled the wires through, circled and tied each bale.

Farm boys kept a lookout for snakes, jumped from the wagon and gave chase to all sighted. Casey Medlin adored snakes and regularly snuck away from work to poke around in holes beneath the edge of the creek bank in search of anything that wiggled. He brought forth water snakes, garter snakes, racers, green snakes, black, and king snakes. He pickled some in half gallon fruit jars filled with alcohol and kept others alive. One day he tossed a live black snake into the hopper of the straw bailer expecting it to be baled. The compressed straw moved along and the snake wiggled close enough to the edge to get his head out and continued moving along, flicking a forked, wicked, red tongue in and out. The man tying wires was one of the street workers and as the bale moved to him he reached to grab the bailing wire but jerked back, eyes great and excited. He dropped the wire, sprang from the seat and took off running to town. He was not seen again from that day and the orphanage still owes him pay.

Casey schemed to play a snake trick against Robert Payne, a wonderful black man who worked alongside us daily. Casey coiled a giant king snake around his middle inside his shirt. At the end of the day's work, on the way home, he warned the other boys to stand aside and he loosed the snake behind Robert. A boy shouted "snake," and all expected to see Robert jump from the speeding truck. Instead he jumped up, grabbed a bushax from the tool rack and took after the snake, chopping and splintering the truck bed in his excitement. The snake and we were lucky to escape with life and limb intact. Casey grabbed the snake and stuffed him inside his shirt, holding Robert and his bushax at bay with his hands. Robert said, "Wuz I you I wouldn't do that again."

We piled high the bed of "Jesse" James' truck with sacks of grain or bales of straw. He sped away to the grainery or to the straw shed. At the grainery three or four boys hitched two bags of grain to a block and tackle and two by two the bags of grain were hauled up and emptied into large storage bins on the second floor. Jesse James was fast; he called for boys to load fast, he drove fast and he unloaded in a hurry. One day he wore out a brand new set of tires because the front wheels were a fraction misaligned and he drove so many trips. At noon he hustled the boys aboard his truck, took them to the cottages for lunch and 45 minutes later hustled them back to the field. One day he hustled too fast and on the way to lunch Clyde Crawford bounced off the back and in his fall grabbed onto a stanchion. We yelled "whoa" and banged on the roof of the truck cab as Clyde's knees and legs gouged on the rocks in the road bed. Finally Jesse stopped. We gently loaded Clyde onto a bed of burlap sacks and took him to the infirmary. He was a long-time recovering and on his return walked with a peculiar stiff gait. From then on he was known as Stiff Crawford.

Some orphanage cottages were heated with wood burned in pot bellied stoves, and others with coal fired furnaces. We burned 12-15 railroad car loads of coal each year. Jesse also hauled the wood and coal, loading the truck with a shovel, scoopfull by scoopfull. Once he pulled his truck beneath the railroad trestle hoping to get a load of coal without shoveling. The railroad men opened the gates. The coal tumbled out and Jesse stood at the side in disbelief as his truck disappeared from sight. He spent the day with the shovel, digging his truck out.

On good days we threshed until all light was gone. We shut down the thresher and rode weary and hot to the cottages, revived by the thought of a long swim in cool water. Night swimming was allowed only during threshing season and we made the most of it, quitting only because our zip was gone. The thought of supper pulled us out of the pool and back to the cottage. For working late hours, those after five o'clock, and Saturday work, we were paid ten cents an hour. It accumulated and was paid out in lump sums at month's end.

Threshing lasted two weeks and we moved from one field to another to the sounds of machines, the creak of wagons, the sweat of toil, and the smell of sweating, heaving horses in leather britches. In 1939 we harvested 6,318 bushels of grain and baled 3,300 bales of straw. By the end of threshing season we orphanage boys were sun bronzed, durable and tough as pig iron. We were ready to tackle something else.

That something else was making hay. Mr. Paul was experimenting with alfalfa and lespedeza in 1939. He sweetened the land with lime and fertilized with manure from the sleeping barn, searching for the best combination to make the legumes flourish into rich hay. He figured the correct amounts of nutrients to make potassium available for the root hairs and ammonia for the nodules to feed the stems.

The hay leaves stiffened with protein and bees began to trip the keels of the purple clover blossoms exposing anthers and stigma and carrying away nectar and pollen. Their prize was taken from them as the mowers moved in. After a few days of drying the hay rakes came. The hay in some fields was baled but in others it was raked into large piles and we did the hot, heavy, dirty work of forking it onto wagons for cartage to the barns.

The sleeping barn and the milking barn had large lofts with a metal track on the ceiling which ran the entire length. Attached to a carriage on the track was a hay fork, with four giant curved teeth for biting into a wagonload of hay and gobbling it up in three bites. Two boys positioned the teeth and sank them to the hilt by hanging on as the bite was lifted aloft. Ropes, attached to the fork and to a pulley on the bed of a jitney powered with a Chevrolet engine and positioned at the side of the barn, carried the bite of hay to the opening in the barn, made contact with the carriage and slid down the track. A boy grabbed a trip rope to guide the load and at a precise spot yelled "whoa" to another boy who yelled, "whoa" to another on the ground and he yelled to the boy operating the jitney and he pulled a lever to stop the pulley.

Hay was a simple crop. I liked the idea of haying, the smells, the weather, the sweating bodies; the harvesting and storing of a satisfying crop. I liked the smell particularly as we climbed into haylofts and re-visited summer in the dead of winter. It seemed a simple idea but we were happy with the results. We grew hay. Cows ate it. Cows made milk from it. We milked cows. We drank milk.

We threshed grain and put up hay and then Mr. Paul assigned Charlie and me to help with silage making. The corn grown for silage was a different variety than sweet corn for eating and stalks reached six or seven feet tall. The bundles of corn were thrown onto a conveyer belt, carried into a chopper and after being reduced to bite size bits were blown into the top of each of three silos through sixty feet of metal pipe. A hose positioned at the top added water and the mixture sluiced down another pipe which was moved from spot to spot by two boys until inch by inch each silo was filled with 120 tons of silage.

Charlie and I were driving a team of spirited Coachin horses, Ben and Dan. We pulled alongside the conveyer belt to unload and the horses fidgeted, moved, twitched, and swished their tails, their nerves on edge from the steel knives clanging inside the chopper housing, the rattle of the conveyer belt, and our own motions tossing corn from the wagon. I was at the front of the wagon and Charlie was at the back. Suddenly the horses bolted, tossing him to the ground and throwing me sprawling on the bed of the wagon. The wagon bounced and jerked as we flew along. I had presence of mind to crawl forward and grab the reins from the hayframe. I pulled with all my might as they headed for a felled oak tree near the sleeping barn. They charged on, hanging themselves half across the trunk and throwing the wagon into a wall of oak leaves and limbs. Everybody rushed to get them free. For the moment I was a hero.

I liked most of what we did on the farm, particularly those jobs where the men, the big boys and the little boys came together to help. But hog-killing was not a favorite time; I didn't like the killing part. Hunting rabbits and squirrels, catching crawfish in the creek, killing chickens, and an occasional beef; these were a necessary part of life I accepted but I dreaded the moment of truth when shots rang out and a farm animal died. The horses, milk cows, bulls, calves, these were all endowed with names. Pigs had no names. In this way killing hogs was different but I still didn't like it.

At the Pig Palace, on a cold day, cold weather was always necessary for the meat to cure without spoiling, Mr. Mont Hughes penned 12-20 hogs for slaughter at one time. We killed hogs six-eight times each year. Mr. Hughes walked up to each hog, placed a short-barrelled 22 rifle to its head and pulled the trigger. I hated the squealing as the animals ran around before dying. When they dropped Mr. Hughes cut the throat of each with a butcher knife. When they were bled out the big boys carried them to the truck.

The slain hogs were trucked to the rear of the laundry to a large concrete vat filled with scalding water. Cuts were made in both hind legs and a singletree inserted between the tendons. The singletree was attached to a pulley and the hog was raised and then lowered into the vat. When raised from the scalding it was swung to a wooden platform, lowered, and released from the pulley. An army of small boys with butcher knives and round metal scrapers attacked the bristling hair, pouring buckets of hot water over stubborn spots. In the meantime, another hog was lowered into the vat and scalded. On a Friday in 1937 the hog killing boys set a record when they killed, scalded, dressed, and loaded on the truck twelve hogs that weighed more than three hundred pounds each in the time of one hour fifty minutes.

After the hogs were scraped each was raised on another pulley, gutted, and after the insides were cleaned out, a stick was left to prop open the belly for cooling. They were then loaded on the truck and taken to Ma Hardy at the Central Supply Building.

Ma Hardy supervised another small army of boys and girls. We cut off hogs heads, stripped brown fat and threw it into a black pot boiling out lard over a wood fire outdoors. Cracklings were cooked out to be later used in corn bread. The cooked out lard was poured into five gallon buckets and stored. Pork chops, tenderloin, and spare ribs were cut and hams, shoulders, and middlings were sent to the smokehouse for curing. Scraps of meat were fed through a grinder and mixed with spices and pepper for sausage. Mr. Paul caused quite a stir on one hog killing day when he lost half of one index finger in the sausage grinder and that batch had to be thrown out.

A year later he was called to the infirmary to explain to a seven year old boy, Howard Whetstine, that he could get along without a thumb. Howard and Carson Carroll were shucking corn, doing their duty, at the Simmons and Howard held out an ear for Carson to cut with a butcher knife. Carson whacked through the shuck and Howard's thumb, leaving it gushing blood and dangling by a few ligaments. Howard took off for the infirmary. On the way his britches started to fall and he grabbed them with his other hand. Miss Rucker saw him coming through the woods and was ready for him. She dressed his hand and took him up-town to the doctor. The thumb was removed but Howard was not told, believing that the splint beneath the bandage was his thumb. When the bandage was removed and the sutures pulled from the stump he looked in disbelief. "Where's my thumb? Where's my thumb?" he asked. Miss Rucker didn't know what to do except to tell him that it was cut off and to ask Mr. Paul to explain how he could get along without it.

I also worked for Mr. Richardson on the vegetable farm. We raised cucumbers, beets, squash, sweet potatoes, tomatoes, sweet corn, butter beans, green beans, okra, collard greens, spinach, carrots, and peppers. By this time, I was one of the big boys, actually middle-size but large enough to be boss over a crew of smaller boys who swarmed around carrying buckets made from discarded milk cans. It was a cushiony job. I assigned little boys to pick rows of beans. While they worked I was free to indulge my passion for reading, leaning against the trunk of a shade tree with a book. I didn't last long in the vegetable fields. It seemed not to be my line of work, or else I was developing a reputation for being lazy. None the less, Mr. Richardson assigned me to the vegetable wagon.

Daily I hitched up Sally, a sleek agreeable mule, and delivered to cottages the vegetables ordered according to a list sent in by each matron. On a typical day I might have a load of vegetables like the following: 55 dozen carrots, 78 cabbages, 25 dozen onions, 18 dozen beets, 4 bushels salad, 11 bushes snap beans, 4 bushels cucumbers, and one bushel squash.

I didn't last long on the vegetable wagon. In September 1940, I was assigned to be one of Mr. Raper's barn boys. Barn boys were hand picked, a tradition dating from the days of Mr. Crutchfield, the dairyman who had developed the Holsteins into a prize-winning herd. He was tall with an angular face and lanky limbs that were clothed in long underwear summer and winter. It was common talk among the barn boys that Mr. Crutchfield slept with his hat on. He lived in the Mother's Building and each morning ascended the stairs to awaken his boys wearing his hat and clad in his longjohns. He was slow moving but time was of importance to him; he carried a watch reputed to tell "official" time. He was often asked about the weather. He knew its peculiarities with uncanny accuracy. Mr. Crutchfield was an imaginative dairyman. He experimented with cattle feeds and eventually developed a mixture that had wide acceptance in other prized herds across the land. The orphanage stories about him were legend. The favorite was his simple method of extracting work and evaluating the effort of a boy. He promised and delivered a nickel for any blister shown to him. Frank Bailey lied and claimed a nickel for "hoeing" when in truth it came from play on the monkey bars. He bought a Power House candy bar but his conscience gave it a tainted taste.

There were many different and honorable duties at the barn and I did them all; feeding the main herd, milking an average of six cows twice daily, weighing the milk and recording the weights on charts, straining the milk, running it into a long trough and watching it trickle down a refrigerated series of corrugated stainless steel sheets, catching it into three gallon cans after it cooled and hauling it to a walk-in refrigerator at Ma Hardy's. In addition to the main herd I fed calves, bulls, heifers, and steers. After milking there were other duties; gutters to be cleaned of cow manure, the barn hosed down and made ready for the next milking.

Sunday milking was a popular pastime for visitors to the orphanage. They crowded the entrance to the barn but were not allowed along the passageway in front of the feeding trough. If found there they were gently guided back to the waiting area and told "Ma'am, you can't stand there. It blocks old Bessie's name plate and she can't see to read it and won't know which stall to enter." It was a common joke and one perpetrated year after year as awed visitors watched sixty cows enter the barn as a boy yelled, "Let'em in!" and each cow enter the correct stall in accord with the names at the front of the stalls; Bessie, Maud, Elsie, Martha, Sadie. Word went out. Baptist preachers spread it. "Those are the smartest people in the world down at the orphanage, even the cows can read."

Some of our cows were famous. Old Katie, registered as Ormsby Vale Eminent Lady No. 1096445, was turned out to pasture after passing her sixteenth year. Too good and faithful to be killed for beef, she was left to die of old age. Over her lifetime she had given 17,600 gallons of milk and 4,411.8 pounds of butterfat. At times she came in fresh with udder so tense that it looked ready to burst. A radio for the barn had been donated by Dr. Fred Day, the idea being that music caused the milk to "come down". Katie didn't need music. She walked in with all four spigots leaking with each step. It was all we could do to catch it before it ran out of its own accord and covered the ground.

Some of our cows were touchy and nervous, anxious to send the milker on a moon ride with a high kick. Judy, a bucking sister, gave up her milk with reluctance but she was a good producer and we hung on to her, pushing and shoving her at each milking, ready to move in a second to escape flashing hooves. Once cordoned off, we pushed her aside and put a pair of metal kickers around her legs. She made life tough and dangerous and orphanage boy after orphanage boy was sent sprawling into a gutter before he learned to get the kickers on.

The barn boys were a tight knit group and many of our duties, such as spraying for flies or dehorning calves were done together. In the summer, barefoot and shirtless, we sat around on barn fences awaiting our turn to cut out a calf to be dehorned. All of our calves were out of prize bulls, Duke, registered officially as Pabst Sir Cascade Duke No. 617461 and Able — Osbornsdale Sir Able Inka May No.726331. Duke was a huge, black four-legged devil and for the most part we steered clear of him. He seemed to never forget taunts and to stand near his pen with head turned away was to invite destruction. In a flash he covered the distance and with unerring accuracy reached a long horn through the iron bars and with a touch sent you sprawling.

We sat on fences and watched with excitement and intense interest as Mr. Raper mated heifers with young bulls. This fact of life was one of many that I absorbed while I worked at the barn. I became interested in the diseases of animals and took particular interest when Dr. Jones, our veterinarian, delivered one of our cows from a deadly dilemma; taking a piece of wire from a stomach, dosing a sick cow with a long-necked quart bottle of vile smelling liquid or delivering a retained afterbirth that was weakening a mama cow. He hated to lose an animal and would often plead with them to get up when they were down. My first thought of becoming a doctor occurred while I worked at the barn.

During my senior year, when my mind had turned to creatures other than cows, I was told by Mr. Amos, our new dairyman, "You are the laziest boy on the orphanage, just living off the reputation of your brothers." His comment invoked no guilt. It was as though he had never said it. After all I was not sure how well he knew John and Cal. Maybe they had been as bad as I.

True, I made a negative impression on Mr. Amos, and Cal

and John had become expert linotype operators in the print shop under the tutelage of Cy Howell. By the time they left the orphanage their reputations were indeed of a high order. I had visited the print shop a few times and had seen them at work.

The print shop was a large three story brick building with a structure on top that resembled a parapet for protecting warring soldiers from the enemy. It was used by print shop boys to play war games. They dropped paper bags filled with water or printer's ink on unsuspecting enemies below.

Inside, during a pressrun of *Charity and Children,* our weekly newspaper, the building shook as the huge press rumbled. The print shop was so different from the farm and dairy, no animals, boys scurrying about, strange smells of printing ink and rapad, a pungent smelling glue that was spread on the edge of a pile of paper and hardened, holding the papers together in pads. The only elevator on the orphanage was in the print shop. Boys maneuvered giant rolls of paper with long iron rods and rode them down the elevator from storage to the press room. At the press the rolls were positioned and locked in place and the paper threaded through long rubber rollers, as a woman might thread a needle, and the run began. Faster, faster, faster. The papers dropped from the press like snowflakes in a storm, onto a stack where other boys rolled, labeled, and dropped them into mail bags. For each run of the *Charity and Children* we used 12 miles of paper.

John and Cal sat at their wondrous machines in a far corner, distanced from the hustle of the presses. Theirs was a scholarly work, interpreting the editor's handwriting and transcribing the letters from paper onto keyboard. Using all fingers of both hands, my brothers brushed lightly and rapidly over the keyboard, bringing a cascade of metal type forms down from the container at the top of the machine. A completed column-wide line of the forms would, by a quick flick of a lever, be conveyed to the mold, where a molten alloy of lead, tin, and zinc would be forced into the engraved crevices in the forms. The resulting product was a hot but solid and shining slab of metal that contained a line of type that was ready for the press. The forms, meanwhile, were

91

plucked from the mold by a long metal arm that put them on a rotating corkscrew conveyer mechanism that released each form into its proper slot, ready to be used again. Meanwhile, other boys arranged the new type into blocks and boxes in preparation for the next run of the paper. The old type was tossed into the melting pots to be used again. When the dirty lead was melted the surface of the molten mass was skimmed and the dross removed.

John and Cal mastered the machines. Their minds and fingers worked faster than the machine could react. John was responsible for transcribing the editorials of Mr. John Arch McMillan, the editor. Mr. McMillan's handwriting was close to that of a chicken scratching and John frequently made changes in the text according to his own interpretation. Mr. McMillan often said, "That's good, John, not like I said it but maybe better."

I was learning what I needed to know on the farm and at the dairy barn. John and Cal were spending their days at the linotype keyboards, around the flat-bed press that printed the paper and among the other job-printing presses, paper folders, paper cutter, fonts of type, and the crew of orphanage boy journeyman printers. They spent time with Mr. Hethcock, Edgar Brock, and Cy Howell. These men were all reared at the orphanage and ran the print shop. Cy Howell was the foreman and the chief cause for a sense of deviltry that pervaded the print shop boys. He was wonderfully disorganized, with lumpy pants, shirt, and coat that bulged with notes like a clown suit. He had a sense of humor that encouraged and overlooked boyish pranks from his charges. He ignored Cal's printing and distribution of a political poster showing a dog running for city council. John was fed up with bed bug bites at the Hutchinson Cottage and brought administrative attention to the inmates suffering by printing and posting about the campus a poem about the bugs' voracious appetites.

Our paper, when compared to the city daily, was not in the usual sense a newspaper. It contained worthwhile articles gleaned from the pages of other publications but was mostly a kind of big weekly orphanage letter. State, national, and international news was drastically condensed or usually not mentioned. The pages had some news for every reader. Each week every one of our 30,000 readers learned about orphanage children and their small doings, when we killed hogs, began planting corn, went visiting, had visitors, etc. The paper reported other doings at the orphanage, which I knew less well; the girls' duties.

Girls ran errands and were often seen at the office, at Ma Hardy's, at the cottages, or at the print shop, but were rarely allowed on the farm or at the dairy barn. Their duties were in the sewing rooms, laundry, infirmary, at the cottages as house or kitchen girls, or at the office or school as assistants.

The laundry was under the direction of Miss Crump and her helper, a wizened old black woman, Aunt Julia Borders, and a gang of twenty-two girls in the morning and twenty-two others in the afternoon. The boilers were kept operating by Mr. Bill Spivey and daily they spewed forth hot water and everything else related to water. On Monday it was thick steam, soapsuds boiling, giant round tubs positioned on their sides, mangles for ironing sheets, and tablecloths and hand irons for the smaller items. The tubs popped, creaked, and sloshed clothes, starch, and soap together.

In the summer, it was bubble, bubble, toil and grumble as the laundry girls stood sweating under fans or sat in windows in hope of a breeze to cool them from the heat of the sun and that pouring forth from the irons and mangles. Dirty sheets, towels, table clothes, shirts, dresses, underwear, pants, and stockings flowed into the laundry in a continual stream. After washing and rinsing, the clothes were slapped around to get out the tangles, pressed and folded and delivered clean to the cottages in a large two-wheeled cart pulled about the campus by two laundry boys. The laundry girls were the largest group assigned to one duty. The sewing rooms had eight girls for each half-day and the cottages two.

In the sewing room, girls snipped and measured to turn out our clothes. Miss Wright tried to vary our clothes so that we were not marked as being from the orphanage, but the girls were far more successful than the boys at this. There were some who had an eye for style and dressed in splendor — as fine, that is, as they were able to do with the remnants that fell into their hands. With a mouthful of pins and a hedgehog of needles, it was remarkable what raiment they managed, considering what little they had to work with.

In the kitchens, large meals were prepared with cauldrons of stew, potatoes, and beans for the insatiate hunger of thirty-five. There was green food of great weight in season and bread for ballast. The bread was special. Ma Hardy baked it three days each week and the aroma from her ovens and greased black pans spread over the orphanage. If we were fortunate enough to get our hands on a loaf, we tore it to pieces to reach the inside with the crust still warm.

In the kitchen too, carrots were chopped like copper pennies. Radishes and potatoes were dipped and stripped clean from their coats of mud. Tight pea-pods were popped and strings of green pearls fell out. Butter beans were snapped and torn from their prisons. Cooking was on a large scale. One girl remarked that after she married she tried to fix grits enough for two, but always ended up with a dishpan full.

The kitchen boys and girls rose in the winter and with chattering teeth sparked life into a cold kitchen stove with paper, kindling, large sticks of wood, and lumps of coal. The wood and coal were in a small house to the rear of the cottage. We ran there and in the dark, ripped dead sticks from the earth, scabbed with leaves and frozen hard. Our hands burned with cold and our minds played tricks of who might be in the far reaches of the darkness. Outside, the world was often white and frozen hard and silent in the moon cold. We grabbed our frozen sticks and hurried inside.

In 1939 the kitchen girls and boys poured up 70,000 gallons of milk for us, enough to float a battleship. They cooked 12,000 pounds of chicken, 150 chickens for a Sunday dinner. When beef was served, it took 500 pounds, and a meal of pork required the sacrifice of four hogs. Thirty-seven thousand pounds of meat went in and out of the smokehouse that year.

We ate 20,000 gallons of canned apples, peaches, string beans, tomatoes, corn, and pickled vegetables that year. Our sweet tooth was supplied with 15,500 pounds of sugar and 6,000 pounds of molasses and in spite of that amount, our oatmeal was never sweetened enough. We ate 2,200 bushels of sweet potatoes and 1,600 bushels of Irish potatoes and pinto beans by the millions.

We were not strong on corn bread, although it seemed daily fare at lunch. We used 720 bushels of meal and 400 barrels of flour. I don't know how much salt, pepper, spices, and the like it took that year, but it all tasted mighty good. We ate well and we worked hard. It cost 68 cents a day to feed, clothe, house, and teach us, 21 cents went for food or 7 cents a meal.

Duty was not all work. In front of the dairy barn in the middle of the day during summer we slid down onto the grass beneath the shade of two maples and tested our strength in wrestling one another. We sat at the edge of the grass and scooped dirt with our hands or lay on our backs and just stared through the tree limbs at the empty sky. At times nothing moved or happened, nothing happened at all except summer and we napped as small heated bursts of wind blew over our faces, dandelion seeds floated by, and the dull rust smell of dry ground tingled our nostrils.

In the pastures, the grass was June high and had come up with a rush, a massed entanglement of species, crested with bright flowers of thistle, coiled with clover and fescue, the whole of it humming with blundering bees and flickering with scarlet butterflies. We crossed the waving green sea on our way to bring in the herd at milking time and if early, found a clear spot to lie back, chew grass stems and listen to summer. Boys and girls shrieked at the swimming pool — never allowed to swim together. The laundry girls shrieked as they piled aboard the laundry cart for a wild illegal ride. The saw-toothed chatter of machines mowing drifted on waves of air from the fields.

Summer was a prologue to the happy, busy fall. Even in memory, there's something special about gathering time that's indescribably satisfying and good. Perhaps the work ethic had something to do with it. On the orphanage all who were able worked. There was pride in a job well done and in the knowledge that plenty of food for the children and animals had been stored for the coming winter. Satisfaction came naturally as crops were harvested in reward for the plantings of spring and the labor of summer.

There was plentiful work on the orphanage and we did it with no idea of fulfilling an insatiable dream or great ambition or even the desire for perfection. Some of us were barely out of the cradle and even these were given a duty. We fulfilled our duties not with the mentality of medieval serfs, but with an eye to the Biblical Wisdom of, "If you don't work, you don't eat."

A fortunate number discovered a passion for their duty that carried throughout life. Many became nurses, many others had their own print shop. I didn't become a farmer or a dairyman and neither Cal nor John became linotype operators, but we learned much of what we needed to know about how to live and what to do, and what to be. We learned the responsibility of being at a particular place at a specific time day after day. We learned to treat each other as we wanted to be treated.

On the farm I saw the complexity of the farmer's life, the range of skills possessed by Mr. Paul, Mr. Richardson, and others. I also saw the modesty and confidence with which those skills were exercised. Each of the farmers had the seeds of invention within him. He did not rhapsodize about the earth and what it took to make it yield but he was forever experimenting; with the soil to make it grow more or tinkering with the engine of a tractor or truck to make it run better. He reduced problems to simple terms "It's broke," and moved with economy and efficiency to find solutions. These lessons made our lives more productive. The bonding between big boys and little boys and between boys and animals molded us into a brotherhood and helped us to be happy, resourceful, communicative, and more understanding humans.

Boys' sewing room.

Putting up hay in the milking barn.

Milk wagon.

Threshing grain.

Miss Sallie and her Olds-
mobile.

Vegetable gardening.

8

Summer

Summer at the orphanage stands in memory as a season of unbroken sunshine, a trick of recall reshaping the past to satisfy our dreams of a perfect time.

Summer, June summer, came suddenly, with the pastures green and the whole world unlocked and seething. We scarcely remembered what came before. There had never been rain, or snow, or frost; it had always been this way. The heat from plowed fields climbed up our legs and smote us in the face. The orphanage dripped in sweat, not from the hot days alone, but from the human energy.

The fields and pastures lay bordered with blackberry, wild plum, and hedge blossoms. Bees scurried to hot white flowers. Birds darted everywhere. Cows lay languid in limpid pastures. Pigs snoozed, lying on hairy sides, backs to each other, legs out straight. On Saturdays and Sundays the mules and horses rolled in the dust, happy to be unhooked from the traces.

The coming of summer dominated our every action, conscripted our thoughts, ruled our games, and ordered our lives.

We streamed from the cottages, we boys less restricted than the girls in our access to the world but, nevertheless, bowed by certain rules governing how far afield we could roam.

Saturday and Sunday afternoons were special. These were the only times when we were more or less free of some form of adult supervision, a point our matrons at least tacitly acknowledged by asking only perfunctory questions about our plans. Usually our plans were vague. Boyhood was not a time of grand designs. We almost always did the same things week after week but maintained the illusion of complete liberty. Our matrons let us alone, satisfied that we were unlikely to run risks we hadn't encountered a hundred times before.

I was introduced to the orphanage woods during duty as water boy, filling and carrying to a crew working their way with hoes along the corn rows of Roses field. When they reached the shade of a huge beechnut tree and sank onto the leaves and moss and yelled, "water boy," I was there. The biggest of the crew was always first, jerking off the lid and holding it as I poured from the three gallon cooler. I poured to each boy in turn, as each drained the lidfull and passed it to the next.

But it was not until I reached age ten or eleven years that I came to know the woods as a place of comfort, where no disaster could strike and where fun was to be had, unspoiled by authority.

I embraced the woods after transferring to the Mother's building when I was ten. The class of 1938 had just departed and the annual upward advance began; seventh graders became freshmen, freshmen became sophomores, sophomores became juniors, and so on.

I quickly found boys with whom I had much in common, Leonard Evans, David Thompson, Steve Batts, and Harry Crapps. We developed a mania for the woods, locating trails, muscadine vines, great trees with low limbs, rabbit tobacco, hickory nut trees, and sites near springs for cooking.

We spent ourselves in the woods on Saturday and Sunday afternoons. With transfer to a cottage of larger boys the pecking order was stirred. In the woods Frank and George Bailey, Doc

100

Baldwin, Judy Woods, and other big boys were in charge. They brewed coffee over the fire at Kamp Kesler Kabin, a log structure built by the big boys. The coffee, bagged in a clean sock, was lifted from the Hutchinson Cottage pantry. It simmered in a three-gallon milk cooler, borrowed from the dairy barn. In the bottom a dozen eggs, stolen from the poultry yard, bubbled.

Middle-sized boys, Cal, Bill Sisk and Doug Procter, had a cooking site near Roses Spring. We smaller boys, Leonard, David, Harry, and I, had a site deep into the woods beyond the spring.

At other conclaves other boys sat around the fire, parching corn, baking potatoes, and cooking fudge from coca and sugar purloined from cottage pantries.

When finished we prepared for the next time, stuffing unused contraband into the milk cooler and in a hollow tree cache or a secret ground recess upending the cooler and fry pan so as not to catch ground water should it rain.

Next, we skirted the edge of the tomato patch, gathered a few ripe tomatoes, walked over to the salt lick in the cow pasture, knocked off a chunk of the salt rock and salting and eating walked toward the apple orchard where we set afire the broom sage and beat the flames furiously with soaked burlap sacks. We always quelled the threat of spreading fire, there were other things to do. We walked on toward the creek and to the swamp.

The swamp was filled with a murky dark-green water-like substance coated with slime. It bubbled with life; rumored to be cotton mouthed moccasins with death in long fangs and slimy leeches big enough to quickly drain dry the blood of a grown man. Boys with ice water in their veins waded the swamp in the hope of catching a catfish or a muskrat, reportedly worth a lot of money in the form of a tanned pelt.

The creek bottom was a world of mud. We stamped in it, bringing it alive, dug in it, feeling for hard pebbles, drew them out and examined them in the palm of our hands. Suddenly, the pebbles cracked and put out claws. We cracked them open in search of pearls. We had it on good authority — our authority was always another orphanage boy — that the crawfish contained great wealth beneath the hard shell. We found only an occasional whitish granule but decimated the population in our endless search for riches.

Heavy rains swelled the creek sending it roaring out its banks, rushing along, carrying a flotilla of flotsam and jetsam. During such floods we jumped in near the print shop, grabbed onto boards or floating limbs and rode them like broncos, bucking the torrent past the apple orchard, over the bridge, to the sewage plant, a distance of a mile or so.

All orphanage boys learned to cut slingshot prongs from the dogwood or persimmon tree, to cut rubbers from inner tubes and pockets from shoe tongues. In the woods and at the creek we always carried them, plunking away at imaginary foes hiding behind trees or floating in the water.

When bubble gum cards began showing the Japanese bombing the Chinese, our targets in the water became Japanese. When World War II came along, we shelled Japanese and German fleets with rock missiles from carriers, destroyers, PT boats, and aircraft.

Caught up in the war news I decided to blow up the bridge over Hamby Creek using a Molotov cocktail. I told no one. I drained the gas line at the tractor shed, filling an Orange Crush bottle with gasoline, looking about furtively, lest I be seen. I corked the bottle with a corn cob made snug with a rag. I bored the corn cob with my knife and poked in a piece of binder twine to act as fuse. I hid the explosive device and waited until the propitious moment.

The moment came on a Sunday after lunch. Before the other boys moved out I ran like the wind to the hiding place beneath the hay in the horse barn, grabbed the bomb, charged down the farm road, ran across the bridge and veered to the left, toward Roses Spring. Crouching in the tall grass I lit the fuse, held it, and at the right moment lobbed it in a high arc toward the bridge. My heart pounded, my ears roared, my eyes burned, awaiting the blast. On the wind there was only silence. The hot air fanned the fuse flame to extinction and the bottle burst on the rocks of the bridge foundation. With that signal failure I departed from the life of the anarchist forever.

Near the end of an afternoon in the woods and creek we headed for a grove of apple trees and picked on and bit into the apples when they were still only nuggets of hard green. We went through three or four powerful bellyaches before the earliest of them was ripe. We also applied ourselves diligently to wild plums and peaches from the moment they first blushed with color.

As the day ended we crossed the pastures chewing grain, talking about no particular thing, pushing through the ragged robins, Queen Anne's Lace, and milkweed, headed for the cottage. After a peanut butter sandwich and a glass of milk, we went to church. In late July and August a million cicadas sawed back and forth in a thunderous refrain from a thousand oak trees, their din for an unknown reason rebirthing in me a wave of loneliness. In church we dozed on hard pews as Mr. Neilson preached his heart out and at sermon's end we droned "Day is Dying in the West" before filing out.

Outside, as the moon disc rose, we stirred to another life. We sneaked through the privet hedge that shut us in from the world, loped away up the road, swallowed in shadows until we reached The Stand, an establishment that specialized in hot dogs and hamburgers. Mr. Jake, the proprietor, sold us vanilla, strawberry, and chocolate ice cream by the pint for fifteen cents. On the return we sucked gently at wooden spoons to get at the richness, drawing out the cold sweetness for as long as it lasted.

Just as we loved the woods and creek on the weekends we looked forward to Valley Nights on Tuesday and Thursday evenings. At the seven o'clock bell we converged from every direction; select boys and girls from each cottage carrying chairs for the matrons. We assembled as a great family, the five hundred of us scattering and reassembling into whatever activity enticed us; games, ambling, gawking, visiting, yearning. The matrons' chairs were positioned on the ridge near the Simmons Cottage and they sat chatting, looking out like generals over battalions flanking on either side not wanting to bother with rules but prepared to enforce them should infractions arise.

As a Simmons boy of the barefoot, short pants crowd, I visited with John and Cal long enough for them to know that I was still intact and then it was off to frenzied play; dodge ball, crack the whip, Red Rover, Red Rover, bum, bum, bum, or to push and pull at barefoot little girls in cotton dresses.

We thought all orphanage girls were beautiful and Valley Night brought out their best; their lips full, blushing scarlet, their hair shining, wearing comely colors, and smelling of aloes, cinnamon, calamus, or whatever the frankincense and myrrh of that day were.

As big boys we arrived bathed, with slicked hair, wearing long pants and shoes, sticking out like thorns seeking to feed among the lilies. Those of us who were sick with love selected a spot away from the crowd and sat looking and talking; savoring the comely countenance and the sweet voice. Franklin Bailey sat with Bonnie West, Bill Sisk with Louise Clodfelter, Florence Breedlove with J. C. Younts. I sat with Fran. At nine o'clock the bell ended Valley Night. We couples got up from the grassy spot and headed for a secret place in the shadows out of sight of the matrons, to steal a quick kiss. Then we separated.

The valley drew us in the evenings and the woods and creek on Saturdays and Sundays but during the week it was the swimming pool. We took to the water like seals.

My first season as a swimmer was like that of other non-swimming new boys at the orphanage. Coach Kearns was in charge of the pool but no serious swimming instruction was offered. Thirty flogging boys, yelling, cannon-balling, belly-bursting, hurtling themselves from the high dive into blued water was alone enough sight and sound to throw me off had I been of the utmost bravery. But, to add, I had never before seen such a body of water held in concrete walls. The pool was 100 by 25 feet and ranged in depth from two to seven feet with walls 18 inches thick.

The first day I watched the others, ventured to the ladder at the shallow end, tested the water with a toe and withdrew to play in the dirt until the final minutes of the hour when my shame at such cowardice pulled me into the water. We were scheduled to swim every other day and I progressed slowly to the dog paddle, float, and belly burst from the side wall, all at the shallow end. I might have got on friendlier terms with the water gradually but a couple of big boys serving as lifeguards solved the problem quickly.

They grabbed me by the arms and legs, swinging me back and forth like a sack of grain, and, giving a heave ho, landed me belly down in the cold water of the deep end. I sank like a stone, touched bottom, fought to surface and bobbed up, spitting, sputtering, and flailing arms and legs like windmills, swallowing, gagging, choking, and thrashing about until I made the ten feet to the side.

Since I didn't drown I reasoned that I must be a swimmer and soon was going off the low diving board, but it was a year or two before I cannon-balled from the tower. The diving tower was a throw-away from a High Point pool. It towered above a row of seven dressing stalls at the deep end. The stalls were for climbing, to sit on, hide in, or dive off of but not for changing clothes. About 1939, Ada Louise Simpson fell from the tower striking her face on the concrete of the pool wall and Mr. Kearns had the tower removed.

Big boys showed off their swans, half-gainers, jackknives, somer-saults, and double flips from the tower and the low diving board. The diving board faced the width of the pool and big boys with a mighty spring split the water and grabbed the opposite wall at the same moment, a maneuver that thrilled the girls but made anxious the authorities who feared a burst head. They re-positioned the diving board so that divers went off the end, headed into the length of the pool.

The water was unfiltered. Each Friday night the pool was emptied and on Saturday scrubbed, and on Sunday night refilled. On Monday morning Mr. Kearns threw in several handfulls of blue copper sulfate rock for purification. But by Wednesday the water was murky in the depths causing more thrill to the game of tag or chase and causing more worry to Clyde Bowers who lost his glass eye into the water regularly. We all searched, coursing the bottom like U-boats. Mostly we were successful in the search but, if not, a wire screen kept the eye from washing away into the creek. Along with the eye there would often be a few pennies, marbles and an occasional snake or frog.

The big girls, so pretty and prettily bedecked for the Valley, were decreed to wear full, floppy, one-piece bathing suits that soaked up buckets of heavy water causing their form to become elongated and baggy. The boys, in passing the pool let their trucks develop a motor knock or their teams became lame or their wagons crack a wheel, creating an excuse to stop. As they fiddled with the balky mule or the malfunctioning truck the boys threw surreptitious glances at the girls who were identifiable only by color of hair, turn of chin, or shape of nose.

We boys were outfitted for swimming similarly, in long hand-me-downs that stretched from Monday to Friday at the armholes and looked black and formal as a minstrel suit. But, caught in anticipation, we raced to rip off our everyday clothes, struggled into our scratchy wool swimming togs and marched along to the pool.

There were not many fat orphanage boys and girls except those genetically destined; swimming and other activities burned off excess fat. It also produced a generation with powerful lungs, developed from swimming underwater. During World War II any one of them could have taken on an enemy submarine barehanded.

The swimming pool had been built by orphanage boys under the supervision of Mr. Peace. It was built to last. In the fifties, when a generous benefactor gave money to build a modern pool at another location; bulldozers were brought to tear down the old structure. They did their best but the walls remained undaunted after hours of pushing. Finally, dynamite was brought and charges placed at strategic spots to weaken the walls. The pool now lies under a grassy plot and we who knew it well regret that the children swimming in the olympic size pool in clear, filtered and treated water are so deprived.

Eventually came a day of lost allure. We gave up the sun and wind of the fields, the illicit cooking of stolen coca and sugar, the wet of the creek, the climbing of trees, the smoking of rabbit tobacco, and the swinging in foxgrape vines. Nature's allure was stolen by the glamour of movies.

I learned it from the likes of Chop Bradshaw and Leonard

Evans; the back street route to town on Saturday afternoons to see the cowboy shows. We slinked along like criminals. In town we darted across Salem Street, plunked down our dimes, grabbed our penny change, and dashed inside, lest we be detected by a matron, whom we envisioned as standing in any of several nearby doorways for the sole purpose of catching us.

We went upstairs to the balcony and sat on the front row, hanging over the railing. At last, lights dimmed, curtains rose, the projector ran through trailers of coming attractions, the Pathe News, a cartoon or two, a comedy short — Laurel and Hardy, Charlie Chase or Edgar Kennedy. Then, came the latest episode of whatever adventure serial was in progress: Buster Crabbe as Tarzan or Flash Gordon, Ralph Byrd as Dick Tracy, The Three Musquiteers, the original Lone Ranger, The Green Hornet. A bonus came in the form of a double feature when one serial ended and another began. The dilemmas of the hero at episode's end fired our imaginations and pulled us to return.

The other balcony inhabitants, boys from the the country and girls from Amazon Mill Hill, created a heady smell of sweat mingled with Evening in Paris. The smell fired our imaginations with fantasies of amour and bravado the equal of those shown on the screen.

Movies of the A class were attended with approval. Mr. Prevo, the owner of the movie theaters, thought first of us, called Mr. Greer when a good film came to town and after they previewed it, set aside the theater for our exclusive viewing.

Bathed, in clean clothes, we marched out, cottage by cottage, the girls in front, not in lockstep but orderly, two by two. We lined out the gate, filled the sidewalks, walked the mile to town and filed into the theater, behaving nicely, lest the matron who led and the dietician who brought up the rear threaten us with loss of the privilege of seeing the movie. Mrs. Prevo was usually at the theater and greeted us warmly. During the ensuing weeks our speech, mannerisms and gestures reflected favorite catch phrases picked up in: Boy's Town, Snow White and the Seven Dwarfs, The Wizard of Oz, Gone with the Wind, Trail of the Lonesome Pine, To the Shores of Tripoli, and Guadalcanal Diary.

In a summer filled with duties, swimming, the woods, and vacation; our chief popular entertainment was movies. We read a great many books, listened to radio, read the daily paper but the movies brought a fresh, new, vivid story that we loved for its rich fantasy, vicarious adventure, romantic emotion, dreams of heroism, the destruction of evil, and the excitement of the exotic and the legendary. Movies made real everything we dreamed of.

We were entitled to one week of vacation each summer. If there were folks back home they sent either train or bus tickets or money enough for purchase. Miss Hattie saw to that. When the date was set our matrons saw to our clothes and on the great day Mr. Millsaps, the mailman, took us to the station. Upon our return he picked us up.

Special excursions out of town were arranged for those who had no place to go for vacation and for cottage outings as well. The farm truck with its high sides was as busy with picnics as it was with hauling hay and grain. We piled in, loaded in our boxes of food and with the wind streaming went to the park at Pilot Mountain; to Morrow Mountain State Park; to Healing Springs to swim and fish and to eat at a restaurant in an old house; to the Reynolds building in Winston-Salem, to the camp owned by the Barium Springs Orphanage on the Catawba River; to Guilford Battleground; to ice cream factories; to High Rock Lake; to the peach orchards; to the WSJS radio station.

Summer was also the time of other things, especially fresh food in abundance. Ripe peaches by the truck load were sent from the sandhills. Those cottages without their own ice cream freezers borrowed from their more fortunate brothers and sisters. One Sunday after church in July 1936, we Simmons boys swapped cottages with the Durham boys. We won in the deal. They had an ice cream freezer and a fresh load of peaches had just come in. We made the most of the swap.

We smothered our faces in the rind of iced watermelons on long tables in the valley. After eating we threw the remains into the air, creating harmless missiles that smacked to earth and on occasion to head. This practice was never judged likely to cause serious damage and was allowed.

Near the pig pens we searched out hornet and wasp nests, taunting the inhabitants with tree limbs. When the winged horde, murder in their eyes, sought to avenge we raced in ninety directions, flailing about our heads using the boughs like terrible swift swords.

Cal experimented with the science of flight by pitching a goose outfitted with a cloth parachute from the tallest silo. He honestly thought that the goose's own appendages would prove air worthy. The parachute was a fail-safe. The unfortunate caught his wings in the strings of his saving device and plummeted to a fatal end in a free fall, a fact Cal regretted as he buried him.

We enjoyed melons grown elsewhere, either donated by farmers with large acreage who grew to sell or foraged from the fields of Carp Conrad, our neighbor to the south. This practice of foraging ended abruptly when Mr. Conrad came out waving a 12 gauge and siccing a snarling German police dog on our retreating forms. Mr. McKoin came down the farm road in his truck, catching every puffing guilty boy. We followed en masse as he drove slowly, lest the dust cover our deep shame at having been caught.

On hot evenings we abandoned the church building and, crowded together, sat on the grass in a little vale between the infirmary and the sewing room as Mr. Neilson conducted vespers.

We Simmons boys picked the bloom and leaves of a plant known to us as sourgrass (oxalis), stuffed it into quart jars, added water, churned it with a poking stick, capped the jars and stuck them into secret recesses in the valley drain ditch. The practice, no doubt a permutation of the art of homebrewing, was intended to produce an intoxicating beverage should we allow it to proceed to the full limit of fermentation but we hardly ever let it go beyond three or four days. We hoped for Captain Marvel strength from it, but if it ever had virtue beyond a vile taste I cannot now recall.

Occasionally during the summer we gave up our beds to church groups staying overnight. We were never given directions as to what to do and would have paid only the slightest heed anyhow.

We knew what to do. Double charged as we were we used up the light to its last violet drop, and even then couldn't go to sleep.

As darkness fell and the huge moon rose we went calling along the horseshoe road, padding softly lest we raise up Bob Harmon, the night watchman. We became his quarry, him a faceless hulk of a man in a long woolen coat of World War I and a five cell flashlight that flicked its way into dark corners. Across his shoulder a leather strap tethered a time clock bandoleer fashion. He punched puctiliously at a dozen stations as would a sentry cry out that all was well.

With vision twice brilliant and hearing twice sharp we played Bob Harmon games in the moon. Games of pursuit and capture. Games the night demanded. Best of all, hide and seek, go where you like, and the whole of the orphanage to hunt through and Bob Harmon to evade in the bargain. Two dozen boys loped away through the trees and were immediately swallowed in shadow. We gave them five minutes then set out after them. They had farmyard, barns, grainery, cottages, schoolyard, churchyard and woods to run to.

We ran under the stars, through oak woods, between darkened cottages, following the scent by the game's one rule, the answer cry. Every so often, panting for breath, we paused to check on our quarry, to listen, heads lifted, teeth shining in the moon. From the distance came a faint whistle or indian cry, a cry on two notes, prolonged. We were off again then, changing directions. Bob Harmon heard too and came thundering, the clock slapping his thigh. But, his duties pulled him to the sites of the key boxes which we had stuffed with cow manure to slow him down. We sometimes led him falsely along a trail strung with clothesline head high but he was wary of this trickery after avoiding decapitation by only a slim margin several times.

In the meantime we were off again, through the waking night, among sleepless squirrels, while our quarry slipped off into another corner and would not be found for hours.

Round about midnight we ran them to earth, exhausted in the valley. Until then we had chased them through all our world, through our jungles, swamps, and tundras, across pampas, plains and steppes of wheat while stars shot to earth and the white moon climbed, raising visions of night and summer that move there even yet.

Vacation. Left to right: John, Cal, B.H., Mama, and Ted.

Swimming.

Watermelon in the valley.

9

Games

The orphanage surged with energy and the playing fields were the legitimate site for spending it violently and intensely, both in the formal athletic program. Our games became a metaphor for how life should be played.

The pecking order set in motion a winnowing. Everyone knew who could beat whom and when the teams were named we already knew who was fleet and who was tough. Coach Kearn's job was made easier by the process. A blocking back at Furman, he was born to coach, and from the unwaked and uninspired he cajoled, demanded, and got utmost effort. The big boys, proven already, drafted little and middle-sized boys onto games as needed to flesh out sides. Imperceptibly, their knowledge and mastery was handed on.

We aspirants searched the library for books on sports and perused each issue of *Boy's Life* and *Open Road for Boys* for advice how to rise to the supremacy of skill exhibited by Red Grange, Big Bill Tilden, Babe Ruth, our own Johnny Allen, who pitched for the Yankees and Cleveland, and our own Pat Preston, who was an All-American football player at Duke and later played for the Chicago Bears. We read avidly to ferret the secrets of stardom and in the depths of night we imagined crossing the goal line after winding the entire 100 yards and holding the ball aloft to the roar of thousands.

We had an authentic playing field that embraced a baseball diamond, a football field and a running track. Football players learned their skills by practicing on a canvas tackling dummy on block and tackle hanging over a sawdust pit at the edge of the woods and a charging sled built by boys in the carpentry shop. Coach Kearns rode on its middle exhorting linemen to tear it apart.

We practiced and played football with the skimpiest of equipment, bareheaded, or in helmets thin as skullcaps, in shoulder, hip and kneepads rudimentary and so thin as to provide little protection.

Our footballs had leather covers and laces that wore reasonably well but their rubber bladders sometimes exploded under the power of the toes of Steve Clary, Hayden Ratledge, and others. Those explosions provoked great general mirth and sometimes even ended the game.

Before the day of Coach Kearns we played football in a circuit of orphanage teams with a few non-orphanage teams as well. The competition between us and Barium Springs, The Junior Order Home and the Children's Home of Winston-Salem was fierce.

Coach Kearns entered us in the South Piedmont Conference. In 1936 and 1942 we won the championship and every year came close. The rivalries between orphanage teams continued strongest but members of other teams, twitted by their coaches at being played off their feet, blamed orphanhood for their poor showing. They said, ''Those orphanage boys don't care if they get killed; they don't have mamas and papas.''

Most every orphanage boy had a nickname and in the zest of the games there were calls for Runt, Spud, Rabbit, Horse, Possum, Squat, and Cocky.

John, Cal, and I never figured prominently in football. John pursued the life of a scholar, Cal seemed not to have any interest in bashing the heads of others or of having his own cracked. By the time my chance rolled around Coach Kearns was in the army, the big boys had left for military service and we who aspired to glory played for a coach who quickly faded into obscurity. I played quarterback sluggishly and am remembered for dropping back to punt during the game with China Grove, the weakest team in the league, only to have an onrushing lineman heave my own halfback into the path of my shoe. For a second time during the same game my kicking foot connected with the rear end of my blocking back rather than the ball. They won seven to zero. My girl, Fran, in the stands, blushed with shame.

Heroes on the gridiron were toasted at festooned banquets to which they were allowed to bring their girls. Miss Edwards and her Home Economics class transformed the gym, bringing in bales of hay, setting long tables in checkered cloths, hanging streamers, and decorating with leaves in a harvest-time motif. The band, resplendent in red and white, mixed Old McDonald with Sousa and majorettes pranced as Ma Hardy and her girls passed home-grown food. Doctor Yokeley handed out mono-grammed jackets and a speaker, often the coach of one of our adversaries, gave an inspirational talk. When the hoopla ended the boys were permitted to walk their dates to the cottages, pausing in dark spots for quick kisses. Such festivity was only for football. Basketball and baseball were not hero builders.

The summer game for us, as for all boys, was baseball. We started as the weather warmed and thereafter played almost daily. After a day spent haying, cultivating, dehorning heifers, picking beans, or at the printing press, we hurried through blackberry pie and on to the ball field for a choose up game.

We played reflexively with flexible rules. If the crowd was large we chose sides by giving first pick to the winner of a hand-to-hand contest up the bat handle. The regulation nine was an insignificant technicality as were keeping score and tallying innings. Most evenings we played till dark except for prayer meeting and valley nights.

If the crowd was too small to make sides we played roller-bat, having a lone batter at home plate till a fielder caught a hit ball on the fly or succeeded in rolling a hit ball so it struck the bat, laid across home plate.

We were casual about equipment. Balls of all sorts were commonplace. They, like the bats, were taped together. Few boasted expensive mitts. Most gloves had pockets so thin that the ball stung like a rock if caught in the center. Donald Harrelson was given a baseball suit with billed cap, and a new glove, bat, and ball by a Sunday School class at a birthday party. Resplendent, he was the envy of all the other Simmons boys who crowded around, eating ice cream and cake and gawking.

Baseball was John's game. He was bat boy several years and pitched for batting practice. He picked up form and grace to go with a good arm. His pitching was sizzling but his heart was in scholarship. His big league play came years later as pitcher on a faculty softball team while he was President of Williams College.

Our big boys, spiffy in official uniforms, played in a commercial league. They were coached by Mack Edinger, Fran's grandfather and the orphanage carpenter. He selected a team from about 100 boys, uniformed them, practiced for an hour after lunch on Saturday and traveled to High Point and other towns playing league ball. Baseball was at the center of their collective unconscious throughout the summer.

The girls played softball but the boys thought it effeminate. One season the big girls schemed to take a crack at baseball. Preferring not to go against the boys, they challenged the men of the orphanage staff.

The challenge was picked up. On the big day Mr. Greer umpired. The men came in work pants, khaki shirts, and brogans and the girls arrived lipsticked and in shorts. They were the glamour girls of summer but, determined to play good ball. They hit for the trees, barrelled down base paths, slid hard in shorts and ended up with strawberries on their cream hips. They added dash and excitement to the national pastime and strove for immortality, but the final score after five innings was 19-18 in the men's favor.

Our outdoor amusements followed a cycle set by seasons and by patterns determined by age and the acquaintances of the moment. Football passed with the mild fall weather, and marbles took center-stage. After Christmas marble mania surged when Santa brought fresh supplies of aggies and alleys, yaws and steelies, cloudies and catseyes. Playing in a circle, shooting out the opponent's marbles and pocketing them, was mild stuff when compared to granny-hole.

For granny-hole we laid out a triangle of holes in the ground set about fifteen feet apart. The shooter started for the first hole fifteen feet back. His goal was to run the holes each the size of a golf hole — forward and back, recrossing the finish line and becoming a free agent without losing his turn. This was rarely accomplished.

The usual granny-hole contest quickly revealed that neither of the two players was able to complete the circuit without a break. They then took alternate turns, facing on each turn the choice of trying to hit his opponent's shooter or aiming for the hole. The hitter got a shot at the next hole and the victim had to start over. A shooter, playing to hit his opponent and missing, stayed put, giving the opponent a shot at his pursuer. The shooter making a hole and catching his opponent's shooter close enough to span it could ride to the next hole, holding the opponent's shooter between thumb and forefinger. The opponent started over.

The free agent, having hooked all holes going and coming, did not have to begin again. He lurked near holes in the chance of getting a game-ending shot in case his opponent missed the hole.

If both players became free agents the game spread out as each shooter tried to hit the other and win. Distances became great and delivery might be made in the fashion of a softball pitch. The game often progressd far from the starting point and was stopped when the bell rang for supper, school, or work.

Not one of us became a professional marble player but this game, which provided little pleasure beyond the satisfaction of winning, taught us strategy. The losing player, if persuasive, could try talking his opponent into a new chance with a simple, "Let's start over." On rare occasions that appeal worked but more often it was refused, forcing play through to the end. Marbles taught us to get along with one another, because it gave rise to disputes over rules and forced us to mediate and compromise. A loss today meant another try tomorrow. We persevered until each won his share.

Muffin was an indigenous orphanage game. Our powerful baseball sluggers, Mike Ray, Skeet Smith, Carl Watson, Hal Warren, and others, regularly knocked the covers off the ball. We stripped the leather, took out the broken threads, restitched, then stuffed the cover with rags, adding cotton from one of our mattresses for buoyancy. Next, we kneaded and rolled the muffin between our palms until all lumps were gone and the balance perfect.

For action, no gloves, masks, bats, or baseball shoes were necessary. Muffin was a handgame, played on a shortened diamond with rules similar but not identical to those of baseball. The baseball diamond was reversed, using second base as home plate, moving first and third bases inward and converting the pitcher's mound to second base.

The full team was made up of five outfielders — three deep and two shallow — four infielders, and a catcher. The game got underway with the batter tossing up the muffin in the fashion of serving a tennis ball, swatting it with his hand, and tearing out for first base with all speed.

The fielder could retire the batter by catching the ball on the fly, or throw a grounder to first to beat out the runner, or hit the runner with the thrown ball before he reached the base. Missed attempts to hit the runner created wild scrambles to retrieve the muffin for another throw at the runner as he circled bases, trying for home.

There were no automatic over-the-fence honors. The batters legged out all hits. Fielders on the shortened and reversed field played near the fence, prepared to dash through openings and dance around as the muffin descended, bouncing through the oak limbs that towered above.

We created a number of other games with the muffin; fanning with a broomstick as a pitcher curved the ball past you, using the woodshed as backdrop; hit and out, a form of dodge ball, throwing the muffin into a crowd that ran back and forth between two pitchers. Each hit boy retired from the game until only one runner remained, a skilled dodger, diver, and darter.

There was one unusually wild football game resembling an anarchic form of rugby that was orphanage invented. It was called, "Bringing-In."

Thirty or forty boys, each willing to tempt death, bunched together as a kicker standing away booted the football high into the air above the mob. There was no fair-catch rule, only a mad scramble. The one who came out with the ball made a heady dash toward a predetermined point, hurtling at imagined holes, colliding, weaving, tearing through, bowling over. It was one against all. If death or serious maiming seemed imminent the ball carrier could quell the threat by tossing the ball in the air, starting the carnage over again with another boy bringing it in. Cleve Wilkie promised the Lord that he would be a preacher if the Lord would save him from suffocating to death at the bottom of a bringing-in pile. It was a serious promise and one he kept.

We were expected to entertain ourselves and to be imaginative at doing so. There were toys, coming mostly at Christmas, spinning tops, all sorts of balls, paddles with balls made to fly back on rubber strings and be socked, yo-yos, jacks, and marbles. But the most interesting playthings came from discards and cast aways

We scoured the sawdust piles at the carpentry shop for blocks of wood, and with scraps of cloth, nails, and string, transformed them into cars, trucks, buses, tractors, racers, sailboats, liners, steamers, and battleships. We plied the waters of drain ditches, mud puddles, the creek, and the swimming pool, raced over navigable streets in imaginative cities laid out in sand, sounding our way with teeth, tongue, lip, and lung.

We armed ourselves with pistols, rifles, shotguns, and machine guns carved from soft wood with dull pocket knives and chose up sides in military games; marching, executing maneuvers, and developing defense and attack strategy. We sounded an imitation of reveille bugle calls through cupped hands and fired on each other, pow, pow, and over the dead played taps.

Discarded wheels were special prizes. Two sets of skate wheels nailed to a flat board became a scooter when an upright with a crossbar was added for steering. We fashioned wagons of myriad descriptions from all sorts of thrown away wheels. Discarded tires were used for rolling down spring hill, a boy curled up inside. To stop was to crash against a tree or to bounce into a ditch. A busted rib, loose tooth or a knot on the head, and other bashed parts were accepted as consequences of the ride.

With the snow we wrapped up like mummies and searched the countryside for a sheet of rusty roofing, a cast away potato crate, or a piece of cardboard. Down iced hills we tore like Mercury, clothes streaming, shouting as snowballs flew thick and the wind froze the wetness around our noses. We slid away the day as cares glided by.

When March blew boisterously in we made paste glue from flour and water, laid out dried weed sticks, lashed them together, wound cord around the frame, cut funny papers to fit, and glued up kites. Rags, sheets, and shirttails, were fair game for sky riding as kite tails.

We sent "Maggie and Jiggs", "Mutt and Jeff", and "The Katzenjammer Kids" on stratospheric excursions as far as waxed cord reached. If the cord broke we watched wistfully and helplessly as our creation floated away toward town.

Cleve Wilkie told the story of a Chowan boy who drew the fire of Mrs. Scarborough, his matron, as he ran across the football field with his kite flying overhead. She streamed out the kitchen door, made him reel in, retrieved her nylons from the kite tail, crammed them into her apron pocket, reddened his jaws with a couple of smacks and marched indoors, paying no heed to the onlookers who rolled on the ground convulsed in glee.

Our games and play produced hurt of the kind that healthy bodies repaired quickly. When tragedy occurred all felt the pain. When one break-away kite lodged on a power line in the pasture William Brown, the owner, climbed the steel tower to retrieve it and crashed to earth in a fiery death upon brushing a live wire. The accident blew all the fuses on the campus and brought sadness to our hearts for many long days.

120

Bringing-in, muffin, marbles, kites, football, baseball, basketball, and their various permutations, toughened and tested us and focused our minds on the future rather than the sad circumstances that brought us to the orphanage. They brought our lives into balance.

1938 football team. Coach Kearns standing on the left, Mr. Greer on the right.

1936 Commercial League Champions
Front row: Carl Watson, Marvin Miller; Manager, Charlie Godwin, Frank "Skeet" Smith; Scorekeeper, Johnny Chandler. Second row: Lawrence Watson, "Buddy," Nance, Pat Preston, Ralph Pounders, "Mac," Stone, J.B. Haynie, "Lefty" Parrish. Standing: Franklin Bailey, Red Smathers, Owen Koontz and Coach Charlie Kearns.

10

Festival

The orphanage calendar was crowded with festive doings. Life was never dull. Our days were filled with work, games, school, church, picnic excursions to interesting points in the farm truck, cottage birthday parties, walks to Kamp Kesler Kabin by entire cottages, bearing food and drink for a hand supper.

Special excitement attended our annual trips to Ringling Brothers Circus to watch aerialists, clowns, monkeys, elephants, lions, tigers, and to munch peanuts, popcorn, and cotton candy. Other special occasions revolved around the calendar: Christmas, Fourth of July, Halloween, Thanksgiving, senior class play, Commencement, and Annual Meeting Day.

Annual Meeting which came in early May each year, demonstrated to us the giant ocean of good will that sustained the orphanage. Farmers, business people, factory hands, and their wives and children put aside their plowing and planting and planning and playing and banded into church groups large enough to charter entire trains. They came in excursions that stopped at our gate, disembarking hundreds with wicker baskets, blankets, and parcels. Baptist brothers and sisters in distant corners tuned the family flivver or swept out the farm truck and on the big day they converged on us, turning the campus into one big parking lot.

For weeks before the deluge misbehaving boys and girls were sentenced to sprucing up the campus. Matrons sent us scurrying to the woods to cut dogwood saplings to make brush brooms for sweeping yards. Matrons hated dead leaves. Every time one and only one blew back the sweeper was sent to catch it up. We pulled the weeds! Five hundred for telling a fib, two hundred for talking after lights out, and a hundred or so levied for the goodness of the soul.

Annual Meeting Day, Commencement, and the meeting of the Board of Trustees occupied five days in the early part of each May. The event in 1939 was special.

Dr. Kinchelow, a well-known Baptist preacher, started things off with the baccalaureate sermon on Sunday evening. Monday evening Miss Myra Olive's thespians magically transformed the stage for the performing of the senior play. On Tuesday evening we assembled again for the seniors to regale us with songs, wit, and corny renditions. On Wednesday The Honorable J. Walter Lambeth, former congressman, delivered the Commencement address.

Annual Meeting Day and the final day of Commencement were on Thursday. Mr. and Mrs. Lord decreed that the celebration on that day was to be a magical event; not a make-shift, rag-bag, or homespun inspiration. This was to be a blow-out May Day Celebration.

Miss Wright and her sewing room girls stitched up royal attire for weeks, outfitting Helen Williams, regal and proud in a majestic gown, as Queen of the May, Della Mae Watson as Maid of Honor, and a court of beautiful orphanage girls, all in fancy dress.

Court Jesters, riding wooden horses, capered around a moving cordon of girls showing off a balloon drill. To one side a troupe of boys in stiff white pants and black jackets and girls in frilled frocks stiffly paced their way through the intricate steps of the minuet. All wore white powered wigs. A bevy of big girls in pastel dresses weaved back and forth in a glow of grace as they announced the entrance of the Queen of the May. The dancing girls held a half-circle festoon of flowers overhead and in rhythm switched them right and left, left and right at about the cadence of the second hand on a clock.

As for me and others of squat neck and solid carriage from the Mother's Cottage, we were bullfrogs. We stuffed ourselves into green oilskin suits with yellow spots and gave off odd grunts as we padded about, hopping all over the campus, leap-frogging one over the other.

At the propitious moment little girls in sparkling dresses and barefoot boys in short pants and white shirts were rushed forward, handed streamers, and started off in correct directions to wind the maypole. Woe to the left-hander who became confused and lost the way in the maze.

For hours we were a blur of color and motion. One event followed another as the band in splendorous dress announced each and carried each along bouncing thunder and a light sprinkling of ginger from the oak boughs overhead.

As the out-of-doors pageantry waned, the passel of holidaying folk assembled in the auditorium to hear and see our best. Robert Honeycutt sang a solo, Peggy Cashwell made the Salutory speech and Dorothy Day gave the Valedictory. Award winners trouped across the stage for greetings from Mr. Skaggs, our school principal. Edith Manney was the best fourth grade speller and Verta Cheek the best of my grade, the fifth. Estelle Hall and J. D. Holderfield received awards as the best all-around seventh graders. Brother John won the prize for highest scholarship in the ninth grade, Howard Day was the smartest tenth grader. John Godwin made the most progress in the band. Alvah Flynn gave the best declamation. Wilma Dixon was the outstanding senior girl and Pat Preston, the paramount boy of the senior class, won a Rotary medal. Della Mae Watson and Jackson Coley received twenty-five dollars each for essays on their lives and ambition. Minnie Ruth Speer and Franklin Bailey got fifteen dollars each as runners-up. Each senior received a diploma from Mr. Greer and a Bible from Miss Sallie.

We orphanage boys and girls had squeezed hundreds of plump

lemons for the next phase - dinner on the grounds. Our visitors milled about, a slow moving, festive, hugging, hand-shaking crowd, greeting each other as they headed for the picnic area to spread feasts on long tables under tall oaks. The centerpiece of each table was a galvanized tub of lemonade with yellow carcases floating in pure spring water midst large ice blocks. We squeezed the lemons and, as well, drank a goodly portion of the ade.

Our visitors wanted to see us and we were eager to reciprocate. They were an annual source of big spending money for the boys and girls. Life at the orphanage required little money in the pockets of the children, and most of what we had was spent for Power House, Baby Ruth, and Butterfinger candy bars. The candy was sold by enterprising capitalists such as Edgar Bridges and Chop Bradshaw who bought wholesale, twenty-four bars to a box, for seventy-five cents and sold each for a nickel, netting forty-five cents profit. Most did poorly at this business, eating away at the profits. But the prospect of big money was enough to persuade us to scrub crusty knees, slick down uncombable hair and, decked out in Sunday clothes, to find a friendly face.

For the price of a walking tour, giving out informative chatter about the cattle, bulls, barns, swimming pool, printshop, and cottages, we usually got quite a collection of nickels, dimes, quarters, and occasional half dollars, enough to elevate our level of living a notch or two for the next six months.

To render this service in an unselfish, accommodating manner and then to receive no pay was a bitter disappointment; even the lemonade turned sour. On one occasion Cleve Wilkie walked his legs off showing a spry inquisitive gentleman every building and site of interest. He received nothing and as the visitor drove away Cleve turned up his nose snotily and cried hateful tears. After about a week Cleve received a letter of profuse thanks for his services and a new dollar bill. Laden with guilt for his bad thoughts, he fell to his knees and asked the Lord to forgive the gentleman for causing him to sin.

After the chicken, pimento cheese sandwiches, lemonade, and the touring were finished, visitors assembled in the arbor, a great rough structure with no walls and a dirt floor, benches, and a performing stage. Gifted children trouped out to capture hearts with stunts, poems, songs, and memorized speeches. The trustees gave their report of the state of the orphanage and Dr. B. W. Spilman spellbound all with Uncle Remus stories replete with Brer Fox, Brer Bear, and Brer Rabbit sounds. Mr. and Mrs. Greer finished the day, he singing "I've got a gal in Sourwood Mountain," "The Fella Thatta Looked Like Me" or other ancient mountain ballads as she got haunting sounds from an authentic dulcimer. Mr. Greer bade our visitors goodby and we jingled our richness, looking toward their return.

Near Christmas there was always hope for heavy snow. We prayed for millions of tons of the lovely stuff, not caring if we were cut off from the world outside, for there was hay enough in the barns for all the livestock and plenty of canned goods, flour and molasses in the pantries for us.

The few days before Christmas were good moments for carol singing and the light of lanterns was all the more if there was snow to reflect it. In addition, the white stuff gave an agreeable crunch to the foot. Carol singing was a special treat for the big boys and girls and those of the worker's staff who chose to brave the cold. The little ones did not participate in it for to take in all the cottages and all the workers' homes meant a two or three mile journey and if a blizzard was blowing the little ones might get lost in the white dark.

At each way station we carolers bore tidings of our arrival, plunging into a cacophony of different words and tempos. But, gathering strength, the strongest voices took the rest with them until the carol took shape and sweetness. Confident, we began to consider the quality and whether one carol was not better sounding than another. Selections from the repertoire were made as we trouped from point to place.

Steadily we worked the length and breadth of the orphanage. Not for a moment did we feel the cold. Navigating by the lights we went from house to house and cottage to cottage, visiting everyone. Children rushed to doors and crowded porches and listened silently until we moved away and then they lifted "Merry

Christmas, Merry Christmas;'' to echo in the night.

At the last stop, the house of Mr. and Mrs. Greer, cookies and cider were brought and we carolers grouped around their porch. Everything was quiet; everywhere sounded the faint crackling silence of the winter night. Two thousand Christmasses became real. The stars were bright to guide the Kings through the snow and in the distance were heard the farm beasts in their stalls. The final song moved all by the words and the sudden trueness of voice. Pure, very clear, and breathless we sang:

"Joy to the World! The Lord is come.
Let earth receive her King.
Let every heart prepare him room,
And heaven and nature sing.
And heaven and nature sing.
And heaven and nature sing.''

Caroling was preamble to a weeklong suspension of the ordinary. Instead, a social committee, comprised of one of the boys' matrons, a matron from the girls' side, a teacher, and one other worker, was busy deciding the events of the holiday week. Mr. Paul and his men sent forth word that a great cedar tree was needed, one that could brush the auditorium ceiling, forty feet away. Weeks before, lists of gift preferences with children's names, ages, and clothing sizes, were collected from the cottages and sent to church missionary organizations and Sunday school classes. Miss Turner went to town on a buying spree for those who had no benefactor. No gift could cost over one dollar. In home economics Miss Stroupe taught girls to make candy and handkerchiefs and napkins for their friends. I made a trip to my "clothing people", the Farris-Andrews Bible Class of the First Baptist Church, High Point. They took me uptown and outfitted me with a new shirt and long pants and gave me two presents to put under the Christmas tree.

As the social calendar began the tempo picked up. Word always came to Mr. Paul from one of our Davidson County friends that a tree was found, and welcome to it. He and his farm crew took axes and saws and brought the great tree in, took it from the farm truck, erected it, secured it, and turned it over to Miss Hattie and Miss Council. They and their crew of big boys and girls dressed the tree in tinsel and glass balls and wound it with a thousand brilliant lights.

Mr. Millsaps, the mailman, made two trips a day bringing a carload of packages and delivering them to Miss Turner. She and the matrons supervised the wrapping and labeling of each package with the child's name.

In 1938 school closed Thursday afternoon. That evening we crowded the gym to see the girls of the eighth grade take on the tenth graders in basketball. Friday evening the eighth and ninth grade boys staged a game. Saturday night was Christmas Eve, the night of the tree and gifts. On Sunday Mr. Greer spoke to us during church. He always greeted us with a message from his heart. That evening we returned to church to hear Miss Louise McMillan read Van Dyke's "The Other Wise Man." On Monday evening the seniors entertained with stunts, wit, songs, and a fresh crop of corn. Tuesday evening was Cottage Night, with one cottage entertaining another. On Wednesday evening we gathered to hear Mr. and Mrs. Greer entertain, he singing mountain ballads and she playing the dulcimer. On Thursday evening the cottages entertained again. On Friday we returned to work and on Monday to school.

I remember the year my clothing people gave me a Kabar sheath knife but can no longer recall the year of the flashlight, the pocketknife or the first base mitt. The remembrance of specific gifts faded but the spectacle of the tree was so intense as to be permanently imprinted in our minds.

Christmas past was recorded in our paper. It was recalled as: enough candy pulling to satisfy a thousand sweet tooths, tin horns with one tone, blown until all became disabled, a knife for every boy, a thimble and pair of scissors for every girl; a year when Christmas, delayed by a measles epidemic, fell in February with the exhilaration the same as though it was December 25th.

Christmas Eve was our choice of days. In the early evening, faces alive and shining, we moved excitedly through the night to the church, there to gaze mutely on the wondrous spectacle.

The tree, at center stage and brushing the ceiling was wound with rainbow and sparkle. Our silent awe gave way. We crowed, chirped, oohed, and rang out, gazing at the tree's base, where mounds of a thousand secret joys were arranged by cottage. Gone from every face, even those of new boys and girls, were the traces of sorrow, despair, terror. There was now only wondrous bewilderment and excitement.

There was little ceremony to delay the distribution of gifts but one ritual was inviolate, Mr. Greer's invitation to all alumni to come forward to be welcomed home and to receive their gift of a Christmas bag. Thirty to forty old boys and girls were always there. The urge to return was irresistible at times of high nostalgia. They came back to the sound of shouted greetings and handclaps, for they were our heroes.

As the alumni returned to their places each matron dispatched two runners to dash down the aisles to lay claim to their part of the magical mound. They scooped up armsful of packages and set sail through rocks, reefs, and shallow channels back to where safety lay. As with a bullhorn they called out, raising the sound of our names above the chaos. They had in their hands the means to appease the insatiate hunger of over five hundred eager anticipators.

Finally the old man himself blustered in, blown by a bullying North Pole wind and coated with color, with bushy whiskers smiling. The gift dispensing and package opening slowed as the true believers giggled nervously, gazed with unabashed adoration or grabbed at his hands. The non-believers gave the once over to the nose, the brightly shining eyes, and the padded belly. ''Who is that guy?'' they asked as he stalked the aisles greeting all with ''Merry Christmas, Merry Christmas.''

Soon he was off to other sites and the darters stormed the stage again, pushing through the discarded boxes and paper that clogged the aisle.

Within two hours the platform was empty. This day that altered the nature of our days drew to a close. Laden with bounty we went home, dressed for bed, and tucked our presents in with us. Humped in bed, making soft gurgling sounds, we lay holding our new erector sets, pick-up sticks, clothes, jigsaw puzzles, and games through our flight of dreams.

After breakfast on Christmas day we assembled in the study hall and Christmas bags were handed out. Miss Wright and her girls stitched the bags by precise patterns from floral flour sacks or colorful new cloth.

Mr. Paul supervised the filling, arranging his crew in assembly line fashion, under specific guides; one apple, one orange, one tangerine, slices of soft orange candy, chocolate drops with gummy centers, silver-wrapped kisses, assorted hard candy, peanut brittle, seeded raisins in a little box with a girl smiling from the cover, gum, licorice strips, a Hersey bar, English walnuts, pecans, almonds, and Brazil nuts. Each bag was stuffed to the exact formula, leaving no basis for a claim of excess or deprivation.

Bag in hand, each boy reacted in a jiffy, eating choice items and hunting those less preferred for the purpose of trade. The scarcity of English walnut lovers and the abundance of chocolate drop adorers led quickly to a gross trade imbalance. Few parted with the orange, it might be the last for a full year.

Trade and eating extended by law over three days. Mrs. Crutchfield, matron at the Mothers before Miss Hester, set the standard in fear that if all goodies were consumed in one day we would all be solid blocks of sugar. The law was enforced through Christmas Bag inspections called hastily at unannounced and inopportune times.

We took our regulation seats for the Christmas bag inspection. Those with empty bags immediately felt stomach tremors as Mrs. Crutchfield stalked down the first row with a big bottle of castor oil and a tablespoon. On the spot she dosed those whose bags were too soon empty. But, as she moved along those with empty bags in other rows began surreptitious signals for help to the already inspected line. All for one and one for all! Apples flew and half-filled bags were passed behind backs in a valiant attempt to save the panic stricken from the internal lubrication. Woe to the one caught with two bags, one empty and the other partially filled. A moral dilemma was created but a small white fib was the least painful route.

Christmas bag goodies were treasured enough to tempt petty thieves to snatch up anything lying around loose and to bring out the bully to prey on the weak. The bully boys demanded the right to paw through the bags of little boys. Little boys defended their legitimate ownership zealously by taking their bags to bed or hiding them in places so secret as to defy memory. Often the peace keepers, at the top of the pecking order, stepped in to set things right.

In a week's time, to our stomach's relief, all the sugary luxuries were gone and we settled back into pre-Christmas ways. The Christmas bags were collected, sent to be laundered, and stored until the candy, nut, and orange trees grew a new crop.

The fourth of July celebration was another festival that brought us together as one great family. Excursionists came by the hundreds from Hickory, Asheville, Durham, and Charlotte to picnic, drink lemonade, watch our swimming and diving contest, and to play baseball. The everyday clamor at the swimming pool was suspended as our best cleaved the blued water, displaying perfect form in the swan, jackknife, half-gainer, surface dive, straight dive from the tower, and double somersault. When the diving competition was finished we competed over and under water for distance. The best performances were determined by a judging panel and awards made.

In the middle of the day, after the picnicking, the hustlers came looking for friendly visiting faces. "Could I show you around, mister?" was an invitation hard to resist; an invitation to part with pocket change but, on the other hand, well worth it.

To finish the day we fielded our first team to go up against a baseball team of visitors. We drew many supporters from their ranks for they considered us as part theirs. It was a fitting way to celebrate our country's heritage of freedom and opportunity.

Valentine's Day and Halloween brought out the decorators and the game and feast makers in each cottage. From their efforts came special days for us to anticipate, participate in, and add to our memories. Some cottages had Valentine ladies who sent either money or the makings for a Valentine party each year. One year the Miles Durham Nursery children invited Mr. Greer to their party and upon his arising after eating to say a few words before leaving the little boy across from him offered a reminder, "We always push in our chairs." Mr. Greer did as he should and thanked his coach.

On Thanksgiving day dinner was delayed while big and little boys rode in the farm truck to Martin's pasture to rabbit hunt, aided by a pack of beagles managed by Dick Mitchell, Franklin Bailey, and Doc Baldwin. Our beagles had such a high order of dog intelligence, so tuned to rabbit idiosyncrasies that seldom was one missed. On this day the racket of a hundred fifty boys insured that every rabbit would be routed from his bed and set going. No guns were allowed, only boys with sticks. I went to these hunts every Thanksgiving for years and if a rabbit ever lost to his two-legged pursuers it was because of grave sickness, a leg missing or a dumb turn to the right when a left turn would have paved the road to a safe haven. Able-bodied animals were outside danger.

In truth I preferred Mrs. Daughtry's roasted hens, mashed potatoes, gravy, and pumpkin pie to slogging through the cold wetness and I suspect that 99.4% of the others would have likewise made the same choice. The rabbits would certainly have preferred spending their holiday undisturbed.

Occasionally there were other festival events in the auditorium, adding to our fun. A concert by the Utica Jubilee Singers, a dog and pony show, a performance by Ilak, the world's largest dog, a seven-foot Russian wolfhound. A circus set up in High Point entertained us with a bearded man with a band of non-stop cavorting clowns, expert jugglers, limber tumblers, a trained bear, a musical seal, and a German contortionist twisted like a pretzel.

Lasses White came with "Mistuh Interloculator" and his band of black-faced minstrels. He scratched the rawest comments from his repertoire and giggled us plenty with cracks, puns, jokes, frontier dances, and songs. His piano pounders and banjo slappers set our feet tapping and our hands clapping.

Our festivals convinced us that Santa Claus still lived, that the sugar plum fairy really existed, and that this was a wonderful country filled with people by the thousands looking out for

us until we could look out for ourselves. At night after each festival
we went to sleep with sounds ringing in our ears and visions of
the event flashing behind our eyes to be remembered forever,
ready for recall when we wished, as at the present.

Christmas.

May Day in the valley.

A Christmas gathering to receive a bag of goodies from the Sinclair man.

11

Hard Times

C onditions in the 30's led to an unusually large number of orphans and abandoned children. The overriding reality was the Depression, nowadays a fading image of bread lines, closed factories, and men on street corners selling apples or pencils. The comfortable insularity of small-town stability withered as the American system visibly collapsed. Order, progress, dependability, and goodwill gave way. The devastation wrought by the depression provided a daily toll of horror: pinched faces of starvation, alcoholism, out-of-work men crisscrossing the country, suicide, murder.

The orphanages of the south admitted children as rapidly as they had space. In North Carolina there were 4,500 children in orphanages and in all the southern states, 27,500. Miss Hattie processed 50-60 requests each month and in 1934 admitted 53 other children in addition to the three of us. Our orphanage had two campuses, housing a total of 632 children, making it the largest east of the Mississippi.

Many children were orphaned, as were we, by infectious

diseases that would now be easily controlled by modern anti-biotics. In other cases there were tales of horror that lay behind the plight of the children.

Several years after we arrived at the orphanage a boy, six, and his sister, four, came from a mountain county to live with us. Two years before, they were living in a camp with their mother and an uncle, eighteen years old. The father was estranged but came often in a drunken state and threatened to kill them. One evening the mother went to the door to throw out a pan of water and the father, hidden in the bushes, shot her with a shotgun. She fell dead in the doorway and the father shot at the uncle as he ran away in the dark. The father came to the doorway, stepped over his dead wife, stood by an iron bed, beneath which the children huddled, put the gun barrel in his mouth, pulled the trigger, and died instantly. The children ran to a neighbor's and were put to bed. In the morning they were taken to grandparents. They were shuffled from one relative to another for two years and, when space became available, were admitted to the orphanage.

At the time of our admission the bank failure had wiped out all money reserves and the orphanage was on a cash basis, paying bills with money donated monthly by Baptist churches throughout North Carolina. Many churches contributed regularly, others sporadically. Each of us cost $20.25 per month to clothe, educate, and maintain; $17.83 in cash and $2.42 in produce and other non-cash gifts. The matrons, teachers, and other workers forwent salary increases for several years in the interest of the children's welfare.

Our daily circumstances were spartan. That it was unhealthy to sleep in warmed air was a universal truth of orphanage life, except in the three cottages for smaller children. The planners did relent and put in stoker-fed coal furnaces that generated steam heat for the little ones.

In the winter when bedtime was called the sun's heat had long before left and the cottages creaked and groaned as their wooden skeletons shrank. We Mother's boys lingered at the pot-bellied stove in the study, absorbing the final molecules of heat

138

before mounting the stairs to dress for bed in dormitory rooms cold as tombs.

We dressed swiftly, not undressed. Blowing hoarfrost into the air, we pulled socks and sweat shirts from closets and dressers, put them on and climbed in, still in our pants. Bundled beneath layer upon layer of colorful quilts embroidered with the names of Sunday school members, we were soon warmed.

We dreaded to hear Miss Hester clunk up the stairs after we were bedded in. It meant bed check. She threw back covers, made us rise in the arctic air which prevailed an inch from our noses, and forced us to shuck down to our underwear. When she left and quiet again abided, we redressed.

Getting up for any purpose was torture. We barn boys hated Beachie, the wake-up boy. He came at 4:30 and shined the flashlight into our eyes until we climbed out, dressed in the dark, and went forth into the polar cold. The urge to go to the bathroom was suppressed until the flood of bedwetting became inevitable. At six the get-up bell sounded for those who were not already up to milk the cows, fix breakfast, or start the fires. They went trembling downstairs in high hopes that the boy assigned to house duty had the ashes cleaned out and the fires roaring in the study hall stove as well as in the jacket heater, a stove in the bathroom for heating water. Our matrons were proud of such hardy charges. "You'll catch fewer colds sleeping in unheated rooms," they said, an unfounded bit of lore passed down year after year.

Colds and more serious sickness were common and death far from infrequent. A central feature of life in that time was the vulnerability of children in an age before sulfa drugs, penicillin, and effective vaccines.

Our wholesome way of life had its down side. The sharing of bathrooms, bedrooms, and living space increased the chance of spread of scarlet fever, strep throats, head colds, and other infections.

Our matrons doctored to the best of their abilities, applying aspirin and Vicks Vaporub for colds and a gummy mustard plaster for those cases where head colds had spread to the chest. The hot stuff was supposed to draw out the infection but did nothing of the sort. But it was harmless and gave the matrons satisfaction that they were helping the sick. We preferred the Vicks ritual to that of the mustard on account of the smell and because it cooled us as we slept.

It was always possible that a minor sickness, without antibiotics to discourage complication or spread, would turn deadly. The inevitable result was an ear infection, mastoid involvement, bronchitis, or pneumonia. Ear drums under pressure ruptured or healed, or became chronic infections or spread to the mastoids. The mastoids were operated on, leaving a crescent scar behind the ear. Girls could cover their scars with hair but those of the boys were visible. Bronchitis and pneumonia were perennial fears, and without specific curative drugs Doctors Yokeley and Sherrill did little except to put children to bed for long periods of time.

The ritual of removing tonsils should have killed one or two of us and did come close but we made it through the torture. A dozen or so at a time were called to the infirmary in mid-May. Miss Rucker dripped ether and Dr. Yokeley plucked away. After a few days of ice cream and soft food the recuperators returned to their cottages and another batch came. Several hemorrhaged until their hearts lost power and they turned blue. These caused great worry in the doctor, nurse, and the big girl assistants working at the infirmary. But miracles did happen, saving them.

Franklin Bailey had his tonsils out when he was a senior. He was sent uptown to Dr. Jenning's office and they were removed on the spot. No one came for Frank and he started hoofing it home, about a mile. Near the gate blood broke loose from his throat. He was rushed to the infirmary and the bleeding staunched but he almost died. It was months before his body had generated enough new blood.

During the winter months the infirmary was clogged with spotted children barking from measles. Window shades were drawn tight to keep bright light from sensitive eyes. Mumps went around too, puffing faces and necks. Small boys were warned against being too active, for danger that the mumps would go down. How that was to happen or what it meant was not explained.

140

Roland Swink and I were put together, with mumps. His clothing people had sent him a bag of oranges. I coveted one pitifully bad and would likely have stolen, given a chance. But I was saved from grievous sin by an offer of a swap. He would give me one orange for five smacks across the bottom with his open hand. I agreed. He swatted. I sucked the insides dry and then ate the pulp; happy with the trade.

Polio scares closed our gates to visitors for parts of several summers and the fear of an epidemic never vanished during our time at the orphanage. F. C. Procter was the only child to be afflicted and he was relatively lucky among polio's victims. He stayed away in the Greenville Shriner's Hospital for a long time but kept up his schooling and regained his ability to walk in spite of a lame leg. Roland Cain, an orphanage alumnus and a prominent Greenville attorney, regularly visited F. C. during his hospitalization.

During the summer of F. C.'s sickness, John, Cal, and I were away on vacation. Upon return we noted the quarantine signs at the gates and were ourselves quarantined at the infirmary for a week. When declared out of risk we joined the others in our cottages and each evening lined up to be dosed with a vile mouthwash claimed to have the power to ward off the virus. In truth it more likely only eroded the enamel of our teeth.

Although we had little awareness at the time, dental service was abysmal. A public health dentist set up shop for a couple of months each year but we could have kept four or five busy full time. Many of us suffered with aching teeth and left the orphanage with unfilled cavities. My teeth went unrepaired through two years in the Navy and three years of college and remained a problem until I volunteered to let dental students at Chapel Hill practice on me. They fixed me up in fine fashion.

There were frequent minor accidents and occasional major ones. News of such events, as with news of serious sickness, flashed around the campus instantly. Toy King found a dynamite cap and stupidly drove a nail in one end, blowing off one finger and part of another. Stiff Crawford's fall from Jesse James' farm truck put him out of commission for months. Ada Louise

Simpson's fall from the diving tower made the headlines. Bill Sisk, an all-state football player, broke his back in a game. Mr. Paul broke his when a white mule bolted, jackknifing him under a wagon bed. The mule was so recently acquired that his temperament was unknown. Both Bill and Mr. Paul were in body casts for three months. Mr. Paul's family lived in fear that the house might burn, leaving them unable to get him out the door.

Clarence Marsh had asthma and one Sunday at dinner sucked a chicken bone into his wind pipe. He was unable to get his breath and turned blue. Franklin Bailey grabbed him up and ran to the infirmary from the Green Building. Miss Rucker pushed in a pair of forceps, turned the bone and yanked it out. He bled, but he lived, and after graduation became a Methodist minister.

The only elevator on the orphanage was in the three-story print shop building. David Haire, peeking over the shaft, got his head caught between the elevator and the platform and pulled it out in the nick of time; a little sore but not cracked. Sam Dotson wasn't as lucky when he fell down the shaft, landing in the basement potato storage area. He was sore but not broken.

One of the Simmons boys found a flare along the railroad track and set the thing off in his pocket by rubbing it during Sunday morning services. Mr. Lewis, the coach at that time, was sitting downstairs at the front of the church with the Hutchinson boys. The boy screamed. The coach, smelling smoke, took off for the balcony removing his coat. He smothered the flames and took the boy to the infirmary. The boy had a nasty burn that healed but left a significant scar.

We were continually in harm's reach from poisonous gases emanating from the silos, from dust given off during the threshing of grain, from the anger of Duke, Abel, and High Point, the Holstein bulls, from other large animals, and, as well, from the risk of misadventure with machines. The wonder is that of all the exposure to hidden or unpredictable harm not one was seriously hurt that way.

There were several close calls with tractors. The first tractors were iron wheeled and cross-lugged with spikes. The orphanage usually had five to seven tractors, including a

142

Caterpillar-20 with treads. Van Hall turned over the Caterpillar when he was waterboy for Lee Fowler, the driver. Van talked Lee into letting him drive it and toppled it when the downhill track caught a deep furrow. When Van became a bonafide tractor boy he toppled again while pulling a corn binder on a steep bank. Ernest Pringle, one of the black men who worked on the farm was standing on the high side of the tractor to add weight and saw that it was going. He grabbed Van by the galouses of his overalls and threw him clear. The tractor rolled over three or four times and would surely have killed Van had Ernest not saved him.

Wallace Hilliard also had a close call. Wallace, one of the barn boys, upon being shaked to wake by Beachie one morning, mumbled, "I can't go."

"What do you mean, you can't go? Get up, it's time to milk."

"I just can't go."

"Why not,? Beachie asked.

"Well, I dreamed I was on the back of Mr. Paul's pickup and jumped off. I was walking in my sleep and fell out of the window. I hurt all over. I can't go."

Beachie let him be. Wallace had fallen from the second story window onto the shrubs outside Mrs. Scarborough's room and crawled back inside to his bedroom without waking anyone.

We lined up to get smallpox shots on the muscled part of the left shoulder. Inoculations had decreased the incidence of smallpox, diphtheria, whooping cough, and typhoid, but tetanus shots were not a part of the routine. Chop Bradshaw got it in 1941 from an unidentified point of entry while working as a barn boy. He and I were good friends and worked alongside each other. He died after a week or so in the Baptist Hospital. His care was the best of the time as was that of others of our family who died from sickness.

We went two or three years without a death and then had five in a period of a few years. Chop died of tetanus. Bobby Godwin and Tommy Styles died of meningitis. Darrell Everett drowned while swimming and G. T. Jones killed himself.

Bicycles weren't allowed but guns were, and G. T. had a rifle.

He had been brought to the orphanage when he was four years old and was a boy who had not made friends. Nearing graduation he had Miss Hattie take him to the U. S. Navy recruiting station but he heard nothing for weeks and became depressed, thinking that he would not get in.

On the Sunday G. T. shot himself John saw him behind the Chowan, near Sunday school time carrying the rifle. G. T. asked if John had seen Leonard Helms: John said that he had not and asked G. T. what he was doing with the rifle. He said, "Oh, I'm going to shoot a bear."

Frank Bailey said that G. T. went to Johnsontown and bought a half gallon of white liquor from a bootlegger, took it to the woods at Gold Hole, drank it, and put the gun to his temple and killed himself. He was buried in God's Acre. A search was made for his kin but none were found.

There were accidents with guns. Johnny Allen held a double-barrelled 12 gauge atop his foot. Someone warned him that that position was not too smart. Somehow the thing did go off, blowing away his right great toe. He recovered and with nine toes went on to become famous as a pitcher for the New York Yankees.

Doc Baldwin peppered Dick Mitchell in the heat of a rabbit race as they were in hot pursuit up a steep hill. Doc, to the rear, holding his gun at ready, intended letting the hammer off but lurched as a covey of quail flushed up. The gun jerked, his finger slipped and the gun fired, hitting Dick in the back and neck. It scared Doc badly. Dick wasn't a lightweight, but Doc picked him up and ran to the infirmary from the Gold Hole, about a mile. Dr. Yokeley picked out what shot he could reach and turned him loose. Dick hunted on for the rest of the day, killing two squirrels and a rabbit. At the cottage that evening Miss Carter asked Dick why he walked so peculiarly. He said, "I fell on some rocks."

The sweating at football practice during August dog days should have led to several strokes but we stayed fairly well conditioned all the time, and none of us ever fell out on account of heat. That there were no deaths from athletic activities is all the more remarkable in view of Coach Kearns' denying us water

144

during practice and discouraging stoking the body with anything containing sugar. "It makes you soft," he said.

For orphanage boys to be soft would never do. Soft players could not dive headlong at the kicker to block punts as Piggy Day did. He was forever getting knocked out by his fearless hurtles but, after all, that's the only way to block a punt. So said Coach Kearns.

On the whole John, Cal, and I were healthy. John had a brief period during which he seemed terribly pale and rumors circulated about a mysterious sickness, striking fear in me. But whatever it was passed and he recovered to be as sturdy as ever. Perhaps it was poisoning from lead fumes as he worked around the melting pots at the linotype machine. I have no recollection of Cal's being sick.

I had one memorable accident during my first year at the orphanage. I was playing with my pocketknife on filled feed bags in the back of Mr. Paul's pick-up. As he started up I dropped the knife and leaned over to retrieve it. As he drove off I plunged onto the ground head first, knocking me out. The other boys yelled and beat the cab until he stopped. They piled me aboard the feed sacks and he roared off to the infirmary. I was soon bedded down on clean sheets as pretty girls hovered around. Dr. Yokeley came, I woke up. He decreed that I lay in bed a few days and I then returned to cottage life, none the worse except for a fresh headache.

I was plagued with headache enough without another insult but the usual ones were of the migraine type, triggered by the chocolate from Power House candy bars. Every nickel I got went for a Power House. I didn't learn the connection until I went to medical school.

The headaches came every day and some days they laid me low with vomiting. I found a small degree of relief from absorbing the coldness of the concrete bathroom floor, lying in a corner to keep sleepy headed boys from stepping on me. Such health curses were tolerated. Medical services were available but the doctor, nurse, and matron were not to be bothered with such trivialities as headaches, unless the angel Gabriel seemed to be

145

hovering near.

Death among us cast a pall for months. We dressed as for church and in sadness filed into our regular places for the funeral and trouped to God's Acre for the internment. I don't recall that Mr. Neilson interpreted such tragedy as God's will. We preferred to think of it as unfathomable mystery. To do otherwise went against a great teaching: Jesus loves you.

Once a year vacancies were created in the big boys' and big girls' cottages by the graduation of seniors, initiating transfer day. Beginning in the nurseries and going up the line, the transfer list was anxiously awaited. On the appointed day those so named picked up their belongings and moved to a new home. Each year stories circulated about old Miss so-and-so at this cottage or that who did such-and-such, striking fear into the hearts of transferees.

Frank Bailey and Pat Preston transferred to the Hutchinson from the Green Cottage and were warned to be on the lookout for trouble the first night. "They are going to initiate you," they were told. They were blindfolded and taken out to the railroad track, tied to the tracks and told that the freight train was coming. It came and roared past: they were tied to a side track. They struggled loose and sneaked into bed near dawn.

Transfer stirred the pecking order greatly. By the time I transferred to the Mothers cottage I was a big boy at the Simmons. At the Mothers there were no little boys but I was not a big boy, more middle-sized, I guess. The proving of who could beat whom started anew, and fist fights were common for a few weeks.

The myths about Miss Hester, my new matron, were legend. But no trouble between us broke out until I made a misstep and got caught after about a month with her. Stanley Sexton and I got into a fight and in the melee one of his teeth was knocked out. The fight was finished and several of us were down on hands and knees in the study hunting for the tooth. Miss Hester came in, singled me out, marched me to her room, and wielded the belt heftily. I protested vigorously.

"I tried to tell you, Miss Hester, that you've got the wrong one. It wasn't my fault. I didn't start it."

She was quick. "Wrong one, my foot! You're the right one,

146

all right. It makes no matter about this time. Think of the hundreds of things you've done and gotten away with. Think of that. You're the right one, all right.''

I preferred not to think about any such thing. That was the orphanage way, getting by without being caught. I could not dispute her logic and the wisdom of that system of justice seemed to be most correct and quite imaginative.

Justice at the orphanage was not evenly applied. Matrons had pets and their crimes were overlooked, but there was no serious basis for an orphanage boy or girl to claim foul treatment. Everyone of us got away with much, some things we're willing to confess, others not.

Life was lived on more than one level of activity and attitude. We tried to live in peace and mutual accord with matrons and other workers, but beneath that surface surreptitious plans and thoughts fomented until the propitious moment. We got by with what we could and lived in belief that we could outwit the matrons.

But our matrons were no dummies and we were often caught. Punishment was swift and tailored to fit the crime. At the Simmons our playing was unsupervised and disallowed acts were settled between the parties involved, usually by fighting. Most often Miss Ballard punished infractions she observed, and we were most visible in church. To sleep, talk or chew gum was not allowed. The punishment was to spend Saturday and Sunday afternoon in bed or write 100 times, ''I will not talk in church,'' or ''I will not chew gum in church.''

Whippings were administered with switches, belts, paddles, rulers, whatever was handy. Stinging legs did make you think before breaking rules. Spud Walton didn't like whippings and got into an unrewarding cycle. Coach Kearns gave him an ''airplane ride'' for his shortcomings and after the coach raised him from the ground with his fraternity paddle Spud would take off, hop a freight or hoof it on the highway. He ran away fourteen times, and each time he was punished the same way. Eventually, a truce was called.

Miss Hester caught me coming out of the movie theater on Saturday afternoon and asked, ''Who gave you permission to be uptown?"

"Mr. McKoin," I lied.

She knew that I was lying and checked with Mr. McKoin. My punishment was to kill three hundred flies. Armed with a fly swatter and a fruit jar lid, I began. The going was too slow to suit me and I cheated by getting a handful of dead flies from an electric fly killer at the dairy barn.

Boys from the Durham, Chowan, and Mothers cottages were regularly punished by making them sweep the yard with brush brooms or by killing flies. The bug killers regularly cheated by stealing from the supply at the dairy barn.

During his first days at the Chowan John was in a fight with Mace Brown. Mrs. Scarborough discovered them and after making them fight until close to collapse she dressed them in dresses and made them wash dishes. Washing dishes was a most frequent punishment as well as one of the most detested.

In spite of a rocky beginning, Miss Hester and I became friends and I toed the line for the most part. Years later I was told by Wayne Young, a Mother's boy after I had graduated, that Miss Hester held me up as the model for others to emulate. "I wish you boys were like Ted Chandler," he said she said.

If so, it was an undeserved tribute that generously overlooked that, in fact, I made it through by the skin of my teeth. By my senior year I was in love with Fran, Mr. Paul's daughter, and we decided to sneak to the movie one evening. I was Junior Assistant Scout Master and was supposed to be attending the Honor Court. The movie turned out an hour after everyone else was home in bed. I climbed the porch railing at the Watson Cottage and entered the building through a bedroom window. Miss Carter, the Watson matron, was sitting there waiting.

This incident was viewed by all concerned, including Mr. Greer, as a grave offense. Graduation was three months away. I was Senior Class President. There was considerable consultation among the workers as I stood in the dock, condemned. Mr. Paul intervened in my behalf. He thought expulsion too harsh. I was drummed out of the scouts and made to dig at the roots of a giant oak stump that stood in full view in the church yard. To dig at this stump was the ultimate punishment; that you had sinned was evident to all. I dug every Saturday for weeks; until everyone thought I had either learned my lesson or that my time was too short to worry about.

I can't argue the merits of the orphanage system of justice in the deterrence of more serious offense later. I can state that alumni of the orphanage scarcely ever were involved with the police, courts, lawyers, and jails because of unlawfulness.

12

Grace

We who emerged from the fires of sorrow and despair soon felt as though we were chosen and simultaneously had the peace of being kept. And it's no wonder, for we came to a place of wonderful folk assembled to live out their faith, caring for us until we could care for ourselves. Our sorrow and suffering were real. There was no use saying it ought not be or of saying God had made a mistake allowing it. But God had made a place for us and we came to burn out any vestige of selfishness or shallowness. Suffering gave us ourselves.

For years during church services we looked full into the grand giant picture of Jesus sitting on a watering trough among sheep, shepherds, parents, and children, one child in his lap and his hand on the head of another. The picture hung on the center of the wall, above the stage, directly behind the pulpit. As Mr. Neilson preached about Jesus, we looked full into the face of Jesus.

In 1938 Mr. Neilson said the following in a sermon titled "The Face of Jesus" taking his text from 2 Corinthians 4:6.

What a striking combination of phrases! The Glory of God...the Face of Jesus Christ. Is any word more characteristically divine than the word Glory? Is there anything more human than a Face? The glory of God — that fascinates us. These two phrases give us the two natures of Jesus in contrast and yet in harmony.

Christ was born as a babe in a manger, that's how human He was. The heavenly host filled the air with song, that's how divine he was. He thirsted, He was as human as that. Yet He told the Samaritan woman at the well that He could give her of the water of life and she would never thirst again, He was as divine as that. Tired and weary, He slept in the bow of a boat, that's how human He was. Yet in a moment, He arose and rebuked the storm, so that the waves and wind became calm and still at His voice, that's how divine He was.

He wept with His friends, Martha and Mary, at the grave of their brother Lazarus. He was as human as that. Yet He stood and cried: "Lazarus, come forth," He was as divine as that. So it is in keeping with the very nature of Jesus that these two phrases should go together: The Glory of God...The face of Jesus Christ.

The face of Jesus must have been very fascinating, and very unusual. It was a human face, yet one that was free from any suggestion of sin or disease. No shadows of secret sins flitted across that countenance. No grim spectres from an unsavory past haunted those clear and kindly eyes of His. Small wonder, then, that that face has challenged and yet baffled the greatest and most skillful of artists. The innocence of that calm and powerful face enraged His enemies, while its sweet compassion, springing from a heart overflowing with love, brought hope and cheer and comfort to the sinner, the friendless, the sad.

Paul looked into that face, and life was never the same again for him. He saw, not the Christ of earth, but the

Christ of glory, the Christ of majesty, the Christ of power. The impact upon his soul that day was such that he never got away from it. No man ever gave himself more completely or unreservedly to Jesus Christ than Paul. No man ever loved Christ with such complete abandon as did Paul. And he longed for the time to come when he would no longer look through a mirror dimly, but could see Jesus face to face. Will you ever forget the joy and rapture of the hour when you stood face to face with the one you loved, and "read life's meaning in each other's eyes?" Think what it must mean in a far higher sense to stand at last on that eternal day and look into the face of Jesus, and behold "His glory, the glory as of the only begotten of the Father, full of grace and truth."

Dr. D. S. Cairns in his book, "The Faith That Rebels" has this to say: "As Paul put it, the first Christians 'saw the glory of God in the face of Jesus Christ'." I remember that many years age, I attended a concert of classical music, and not having any adequate understanding of its greatness, I was feeling rather weary of it, and my attention was wandering. Then my eyes fell on the face of a man sitting near me. I was startled, for his face was transfigured as by an inner light, and his eyes were shining. He seemed like one carried beyond all fear and care and sorrow. It was quite impossible for me to doubt that he was hearing things I could not hear. I saw the light of the knowledge of the glory of music on his face so that for a moment I could see what it was, though I could not hear what it was." Something like this was the experience of those early Christians who so caught the glory of the Master, that the world about them "took knowledge that they had been with Jesus."

Does the world take such knowledge of us, or does the world take knowledge of us that we have been with self, or with sin, or with worldly pleasure: O may we live in such close fellowship with Jesus, that we shall catch some

of the radiance of that glory, the glory of God in the face
of Jesus Christ, and reflect it to those who "sit in darkness and in the shadow of death."

Mr. Neilson was born in Sicily of Scottish Missionary parents.
In the faintest of Scottish brogue he delivered believable sermons of Jesus' love. He knew his work and he believed and he
loved his belief. We knew that to choose Christianity as a way
of life was a serious and high-minded decision. Most of us did
so choose to follow Jesus and were baptized into the Church.

Church was a constant in our lives. We attended often.
Church-going was a form of social intercourse, a habit, a social
custom, an occasion when we put on our Sunday clothes, went
to Sunday school and church and afterwards sat down to the largest meal of the week. Neither mood nor inclination had any say
in the matter. Only bed-confining illness kept us away from
church.

But we acquired more than the trappings of social habit. The
face of Jesus was made real in the fidelity of those who spent
their lives at the orphanage as matrons, teachers, and workers.
It was made real by the thousands outside our boundaries in small
and large enclaves who shared their goods with us. It was made
real in the lives of those who finished their time in the orphanage and departed into the world; by their faithfulness to what
they had been taught.

Admittedly, some of the sermons had a pronounced Baptist
flavor, leading naturally to a decided partisanship in our religion.
In our minds Heaven flowed with much water and once, in an
argument over whether Methodists and Presbyterians could be
admitted, Jerry Griffin piped up, "I'm Baptist bred, I'm Baptist
born and when I die I'll be Baptist gone."

We were unconcerned with theological niceties or even
theology itself, and the fine points of denominational distinction
were lost on us. We did, as Baptists, baptize by immersion and
there were other conventions we followed that were determined
by denominational custom. But our religious instruction, while
specifying certain absolutes of belief and conduct, was not severely
restrictive in our daily lives or in our learning about the world.

It was required of us that we honor those periods set aside for worship. We did understand courage, toughness, and fidelity and saw these not only in the orphanage workers but also in the stream of missionaries visiting from foreign lands. But, once Sunday school, church, and dinner were past, we were allowed more freedom than usual for the rest of the day because duties did not call.

There were a few vestiges of a stricter past. Prohibitions against football and baseball on Sunday afternoon fell gradually, and by our time these activities were accepted as normal parts of civilized life.

Mrs. Crutchfield and a few other matrons were exemplars of Victorian Puritanism. To her, reading the Sunday paper was a deadly sin. She stashed the *News and Observer* in a corner until Monday. She snooped around and swooped down on us if we were reading sports magazines, westerns, or romantic pap. Unholy and ungodly writings were taboo on Sunday.

Mrs. Crutchfield expected boys to move in angelic silence with dour countenance on Sunday. If caught playing ball or marbles, the instruments of sin were confiscated and we were sent inside to sit, pray, and to meditate on errant ways until supper time. The only safe course around Mrs. Crutchfield was to sit quietly and read the Bible. Few did. On Monday all religious fervor slid away as we struggled, pushed, tugged, and tore at each other for funnies and sports pages.

We were expected to give up childish ways in church. Poking, pushing, throwing spitballs, passing notes, and munching were not allowed. We were not only punished with a stern look, but if sitting close to the matron received a pinch or a slap. If the rule breaking was serious we were sent off to bed after Sunday dinner, required to write a correcting or reminding sentence up to a thousand times or sent off on a fly killing binge.

We were not a prosperous flock and gave no oyster suppers, had no bingo, bazaars, or rummage sales, but when the offering plate was passed we put in of what we had. We retained funds to pay Mr. Neilson and to operate the church. But the rest went to further other good causes: a woman's training center in Canton,

155

China; Dr. George Green's surgical work in Nigeria; Red Cross relief work; the Baptist Hospital; a good will center in Tabata, Japan. The combination of offerings for causes throughout the world and sermons by visiting foreign missionaries gave us a global awareness.

Upon reaching adolescence most of us attended the Baptist Young People's Union and the Royal Ambassadors or the Girl's Auxiliary. I never got heartily involved in either organization. Rather, I found the proceedings quite boring and sat around doing what some of the others were doing at the time, squirming in our seats. Talk in a lighter vein with a touch of adventure did appeal to me. Mr. Eggers, the seventh grade teacher, became a Royal Ambassador leader and thrilled us with his accounts of adventures flying his own plane. When the war came along he signed up and later was lost in a bombing raid on Tokyo. Some found these organizations quite rewarding. Milton Bliss and John Brinegar were awarded blue and gold silk capes, signifying their progress toward the coveted Ambassador Plenipotentiary.

Some of our adult fellow christians, or matrons and other workers, were quite stern. But others, also all christians, were witty and merry, never ostentatiously carrying Bibles to impress, never shouting "Praise the Lord," or quoting scripture to point a moral. We became more like the latter, cheerful Christians, detoured from the road to Death Row by the Holy Spirit and Jesus' love.

It was through Mr. Neilson, Mr. Paul, Miss Sallie, our teachers, and matrons that the Holy Spirit showed us the light. They were the chief means but there were others, all operated through human kindness and friendship.

Come spring, hundreds of farmers had us on their minds as they looked at the heavens and sifted soil, hitched up their mules, and began to plow. Children and their mothers stitched pillow cases, quilted, and made ready for the work to be done come fall and harvest time.

Mr. J. A. Ruth organized a potato club in Marion. In Boone farmers set aside a God's Acre to work and plant for our benefit. Children begged to plant pumpkin seeds in their fathers' and grandfathers' corn fields.

During the entire year there were gifts of money, clothing, Octagon soap coupons, quilts, handkerchiefs, bath items. The folks of First Baptist Church of Cliffside sent a bale of towels and washcloths; a monogrammed set for each child. The True Trusted Tried Sunday School class of the Allen Street Church of Charlotte sent handkerchiefs. The Busy Bee girls of Hocutt Memorial Church sent clothes and towels for the Mitchell girls. Circle number eight of Greensboro's First Baptist sent jelly and preserves to the Miles Durham children. The Waughtown "Lend a Hand" club sent thirty sun suits to the Fleming girls, one for each child. In 1938 Miss Turner collected 26,000 Octagon soap coupons and exchanged them for $100.00. Reverend Fred Day sent a radio to the barn boys so that they could hear the football games while working.

Y. W. A.s and G. A.s of Kannapolis sent Miss Ballard eleven bed spreads for our beds. Mr. Howard Weaver of Fork came by to tell Mr. Paul that he had a good horse, almost a member of his family, and that he wanted to give it for farm use. Mr. Paul found the big black horse to be gentle and put him to the one-horse wagon for delivering milk and vegetables. Mr. Price Knowle's farm hands picked and sent 464 quarts of strawberries for pies, shortcake, and jam.

So many quilts had been sent over the years that a call went out: "Quilts make most acceptable gifts but, ladies, we really have all of the double bed quilts we will ever need. We do not use double beds anymore. Every child has his own bed and it is a single bed. As a matter of fact, our stock of quilts is sufficient for several years to come. We have about 1,000 new ones. That sounds big but after all it is only about two to a child, but they will last for many years to come."

Camilla Maynard was quite ill and put to bed for months. The other girls at the Downing Cottage started a move to collect money enough to buy a radio for her. Enough soon came and the radio was installed. One donor wrote a letter to Mr. Covington, our treasurer:

Dear Bro. Covington:

November 4, 1931, I went to the hospital for a rest. The doctor said a few days would put me in shape. Six months in the hospital and then carried from wife and children to a strange place called the N. C. Sanatorium where I spent sixteen months among strangers. But thanks for one who will never forsake us if we will only trust him, last week I was permitted to do some light work, for which I received pay Saturday. This being my first pay day since November 4, 1931. Sunday as I was reading Charity and Children and saw where this girl had to take a rest I said only them that are sick or have been sick know what it is to be carried away in a strange land among strange people. So I am sending one dollar of my pay to help buy this girl a radio. Please give it to the Downing girls from an humble sinner.

My Dear Little Friends:

In July I was operated on for appendicitis at the Wilkes hospital. Mama wanted to send the first quilt blocks I ever pieced to you. The ladies said no, let's make another quilt for them. I think it's a nice quilt and hope when you look at it you'll think of me.

I too am an orphan, 11 years old; in the sixth grade. Live two miles from school. In bad weather I stay with one of mama's friends near the school. My mama is a Christian, has worked so hard on the farm to raise her five children, the two oldest are married. I'm the youngest.

Papa died when I was less than one year old but grandpa Walker has been a father to me.

Mama has rheumatism, sometimes she can't walk. Now she can't use her right hand.

I like to read *Charity and Children,* hope some time I'll be able to subscribe.

My name is

Johnie Maia Boyd,
R.F.D. 2, Ronda, N.C.

Campbell College
Buies Creek, N.C.
December 2, 1943

Dear Brother Covington:

I hope you will feel that the story given below merits publication in Charity and Children.

Contained in this offering from our church is $35.00 from Angel Aguilera, ministerial student here at Campbell from Cuba. I want to tell you this story of how a pennilcss boy from a forcign land camc to givc $35.00 to orphans in North Carolina.

On the day before Thanksgiving, we had a special prayer in all our Bible classes that the faculty and students might make a worthy offering the following day for the Orphanage. Aguilera was in one of those classes. We knew that our Cuban classmate was praying, but none of us was aware of the earnestness with which he prayed. And none of us was conscious of the compassion the Lord had given him for the underprivileged in our own land.

The next morning at ten-thirty, students, teachers, and community people gathered in the spacious and beautiful D. Rich Memorial Auditorium for the annual Thanksgiving service. With President Leslie Campbell in charge, we sang hymns, read scripture, offered prayers, and then scores of us stood up one by one to tell God's goodness to us during the past year. Then came the offering, preceded by the passing of envelopes and the lovely picture-folders describing some of the things Baptists are doing at Thomasville and at Kennedy Home. And all the while Angel's burden of prayer was growing heavier and his compassion deeper. He had not a penny to give. How could he help? Having prayed so earnestly for this cause,

159

he must find a way to do something about it. He had heard of people giving their jewels to the Lord...Into the envelope went the most prized possession he had on earth, a handsome Waltham watch which he and his brothers had been able to buy in Cuba at a sacrifice price ($13.00). He didn't even keep the lovely gold chain attached to it!

Nobody knew that such an offering had been made until later when, in his home, our church treasurer found the stuffed, heavy, queer-looking envelope inscribed "Angel Aguilera." He could hardly believe his eyes when he saw the contents.

In the service Sunday morning somebody said softly to the pastor, "Let's buy that watch back from the Orphanage, give it back to Aguilera, and send the amount it is worth to the Orphanage in his name." The Treasurer and Chairman of deacons felt the same way about the matter. So at the close of the service, Brother Marshbanks exhibited the watch and told briefly the story of its dedication to the Orphanage. The ushers passed the plates and, even though our people had already given several hundred dollars that morning to at least three different offerings, this offering amounted to nearly $35.00. So, if you think this is a fair price for the watch, Brother Covington, we are returning it to its former owner and sending you $35.00 for Angel Aguilera.

Yours in Christ,
Chas. B. Howard

Come September the trucks began rolling in. In 1938 Mr. Willie Cook of Mt. Vernon singing clan brought 1600 pounds of cabbage. Quickly to follow were eight trucks of produce from the churches of Yancey County. Next a box car load of produce came from Macon, Tennessee, and Tuckaseigie Associations. Mr. W. O. Reddick brought a truck load of apples. Truck after truck we unloaded into our storage houses. In 1938 the canned goods we received were estimated to be worth $8,000.00.

The net of kindness and friendship was widespread and hard to imagine but the importance of the gifts of good people to our

160

existence cannot be exaggerated.

At an early age we learned to be genuine in our appreciation. It was asked of quite a number of us that we express that appreciation as, in the company of Mr. Greer, we traveled to speak in distant churches. It was always a great pleasure to be in his company. Those with singing voices, John Brinegar, Milton Bliss, Eloise Stancil, Lib Rollins, and many others were organized into trios and quartets. John and Cal had their time of making speeches and as I came along so did my opportunities.

On December 4, 1938 I went with Mr. Greer to the First Baptist Church of Gastonia to give a speech. Weeks before I sat in the study at the Simmons and tried to put my thoughts on paper. It was hard going. I thought of my earlier days, days at Holland Creek and Black Mountain. I thought of my parents, Aunt Gus, B. H., and of my friends in Black Mountain. I wrote down my feelings and impressions about my four years in the orphanage.

Shrinking from misery, I walked to the stage that Sunday morning in front of hundreds of people. Too short for the podium, I stood to the side and began my speech with knees trembling and voice shaking. Otherwise it was a flawless performance and I walked to my seat feeling smooth and satisfied. We rode home through the red of twilight, the engine humming and me sleepy on the seat with Mr. Greer. He let me out at the Simmons and I was soon in bed, my head ringing with sleep, my ears full of motors and hymns. My shut eyes were printed with the images of the day, the crowds in the church, and of my speech.

My most vivid impression now is of Saturday evening. We had spent the night with one of Mr. Greer's friends, and at supper were fed pineapple, the first I had ever tasted. I could not get enough of it. Later, we went to town and while in Rose's store I became sick and vomited. I was afraid to tell anyone I was sick, a fact that quickly, and in a humiliating fashion, became well-known to a crowd of onlookers.

I guess my conduct and performance were good enough for Mr. Greer in spite of the incident in the dime store. The next week I went with him and made the speech again to thousands at the annual meeting of the North Carolina Baptist State Convention.

Mr. Neilson with two senior girls.

The church.

13

Workers

The goodness of the matrons and other workers overcame the evil consequences of the circumstances that made us orphans. It was an act of grace that they be there, in that place, at that time. But, that meaning of our experience was not so well understood when we were in the orphanage.

As children we mapped out our lives with special care when we were watched like hawks, whether in school or at the cottage, anytime we were in the presence of an adult. On the surface we tried to move in accord with the wishes of the workers, so as to keep peace. Beneath the surface there simmered a will to test wits against the workers, to see what we could get by with, without being caught. But, workers were not dummies. Our matrons knew far more than they let on and they allowed us to test the limits, so long as our behavior didn't do large or permanent damage. In this way each worker at the orphanage helped shape each child's turn of mind, way of thinking, attitude, and approach to life.

As children we also learned from one another. But the scope, style, form, and content of our learning was affected as a group by our relationship with the workers. We were blessed with a remarkable balance between adequate unsupervised free and unstructured time and time with adults in supervised activities. Each of us shared strong bonds of common experience; some with a matron, some with a teacher, some with Mr. Paul or Miss Sallie, or Mr. Greer. It was with that special one that we lived through the frustrations and predicaments of powerlessness and ignorance and from them drew the wisdom to prevent stupid and sometimes grave bungles.

The relationship with matrons helped develop a sense of belonging. It was not the same for any two children. I would not have traded Miss Hester for any other matron and when I transferred to the Watson cottage there were boys there — Wallace Maultsby, John Brinegar, Milton Bliss—who felt as strongly about Miss Carter. But, Miss Carter and I were always at war over my testing and her rules enforcement.

Miss Carter, Miss Hester, Mrs. Fox, Mrs. Frazier, Mrs. Scarborough, Mrs. Wysong, Miss Ballard. Mrs. Garrett, Mrs. Barbee, Mrs. Chatham, Miss Daughtry, Miss Doughton, Mrs. Nipper, Mrs. Britton, Miss Hedgecock, Miss Faircloth, Mrs. Henry, Mrs. Smith, Swannie McHargue, Mrs. Hilliard. These were the stalwart matrons during our day. Their characteristics were: fidelity in role, longevity in service, and camaraderie in association. They had a good time together.

Occasionally an unsuitable person was employed as a worker. A seventh grade teacher of the 40's punished children with a forceful backhand slap and other acts of unrestrained might. A crisis erupted when Bob Tate faced him and threatened him. Mr. Greer had the man and his wife removed within 24 hours.

In the November 23, 1888, issue of *Charity and Children* the following advertisement appeared:

Wanted

A matron for the Biggs family. She should be pious and industrious and free from all vices against which we warn children. She should understand keeping a house in order, cutting and making clothes and the proper preparation of the different kinds of food; she should know how to milk, make cheese and prepare butter for the table; she should know how to raise chickens, how and when to plant vegetables, and how to save seeds; how to make soap, to make it good, and to use it when made. Girls in their teens and women who use intoxicating liquors, opium or tobacco are requested not to apply.

Address, J. H. Mills,
Thomasville, N. C.

In our time matrons no longer made clothes, milked cows, made cheese and butter or tended garden. Still the odds and ends of earlier eras were like parts of a connected frieze. For each year, in each child, the contributions made by matrons, teachers, workers at the dairy, farm, print shop, sewing room, and laundry, were parts of a whole. Each year the parts that made up the whole were a little different than those of the preceding year and of the one to come. This is why, when we gather for homecoming, there is no end to the stories of how life was at the orphanage.

Becky Greene and Nell Deaton, working with Ma Hardy, were told by Ralph Pounders that Mrs. Hilliard kept a jug of iced water on the shelf of the walk-in freezer. On a hot afternoon Nell slipped in several times for a sip or two. Her stomach began to pain and she developed a running off severe enough for a trip to the infirmary. Miss Rucker quizzed her. "I just drank some water," Nell said. Miss Rucker found out that the water was "Crazy Water Crystals," Epsom salts.

A Mrs. Wilson, a tall shapeless woman who loped like a giraffe and always wore white, was for a time in the late 30's a matron at the Downing cottage. She gathered her thirty-five charges after church on Sunday evenings and went walking outside the campus. As they neared the railroad tracks she insisted on the girls waiting while she used her flashlight to see if a train was coming.

Squirreling away food to eat under cover of darkness and under bed sheets was a favorite pastime in the girls' cottages. It was sometimes a hot dog with chili and onions from Jake's stand, or wormy chestnuts from the mountains (worm holes were not seen

165

in the dark). Sometimes it was a jar of peaches or a jar of cherries, or a loaf of bread, the center stuffed with peanut butter. Whatever it was had to be eaten entirely as there was no place to hide the remains.

Connie Duncan, Edith Bowers, and others, hid a huge sweet potato for after hours. Bunched together in one bed under cover, they laughed and passed and bit into the tuber with one after another acting as lookout for Mrs. Britton. The signal was a coughing spell. Sure enough, Mrs. Britton heard the commotion when Connie was the sentry. Connie coughed long and loud and the crowd scattered to their own beds. Mrs. Britton took Connie to her room. When she returned the others crowded round, "What'd she do? What happened?" they chorused as Connie wiped her mouth.

"She gave me a dose of Milk of Magnesia, thought I was coming down with a cold."

John caught Mrs. Scarborough's ire. She claimed that he was bullying another boy. He denies it still, of course. Bullying and tattling were forbidden. Punishable crime had to be detected by the matron, the teacher, or other worker.

As for fighting, much of it was out of sight of the adults, thus the burning issues were settled without recourse to grown-up wisdom. With Howard Day and Grady Thomas it was forever fussing and scrapping, scrapping and fussing, until Miss Scarborough was fed up. One day, during a contest of knockdown and roll around on the ground, she took a stick and led them to the ball field behind the Chowan. She made them fight, and fight, and fight, until both were ready to drop, but if they slowed or stopped, she set upon them with the stick. She laid it on and forced them to lay it on until there was no more fight left in either. Thereafter they lived in peace.

Two-gun Burleson came to the Miles Durham in 1936. He was four years old. His first days were unhappy, he couldn't stop crying. His points of reference to his former existence were a harmonica and a snow suit which he wore continually, even to bed. But, he wet the bed, causing Mrs. Bannister to strip him of the suit and wash him in a tub of cold water, as was her custom for this offense. There were variations in the punishment of this misdeed; dipping face and head beneath cold water in a basin, making threats to cut off the offending genital with a butcher-knife. She took his snowsuit, took his harmonica presumably because it was too noisy — and forced him to spend a day alone in the darkness of the furnace room.

Even when Two-gun was twelve and at the Mothers cottage he was still unhappy and ran away three or four times. Once he and Dude Stanley sneaked out the gate and hit the road to Wallburg, hitching a ride with a farmer on his wagon. In Wallburg their benefactor let them down and gave them a dollar each.

The money didn't last. They were headed for Elkin. They slept under bushes and ran from German police dogs. Finally, they reached the house of Dude's sister. But, when he knocked the occupants were strangers.

"Is this Elsie Stanley's house?" Dude asked.

"Honey, she's been gone ten years," the woman answered. The woman took them in and fed them.

How many eggs can you eat?" she asked Two-gun.

"Six," he replied.

When these were gone, he asked, "Can I have six more?"

The woman got the story from the boys and called a preacher, who brought an angel food cake. Miss Hattie was called. She came, loaded them up and drove them back to the orphanage.

Running away scarcely ever succeeded but boys tried it time after time, often after an insignificant something or as a consequence of general discontent. Spud Walton and Harold Shaver each ran away fourteen or fifteen times. I never knew of a girl running away, but some probably did or wished to.

Dwight West, Lynn Hammond, and Maurice Owen ran away, only to be caught by the police in Lexington and returned by Mr. McKoin. They were punished by having to dress in girl's clothes; Dwight in a pink and white checkered dress and Lynn and Maurice in long yellow garb. Each had long blue bloomers or teddies. Dwight, in the third grade, was embarrassed and kept his head on the desk all day. Maurice, in the fifth grade, hurled himself into a football game at recess, throwing his legs in the teddies

167

high in the air as he lay on his back.

Boys were not beyond playing tricks on matrons. George Bailey rigged a pan of marbles above a dormitory door at the Hutchinson. Mrs. Edwards, making bed check, jarred the pan loose. The marbles rained down and she slipped and slid as she made her way down the stairs.

Casey Medlin hid two half gallon fruit jars filled with alcohol-preserved snakes beneath the quilts at the Chowan. Mrs. Scarborough, passing out cover at winter's onset, almost died as she realized what the jars contained. She made Casey bury them beneath the sawdust in the tackling pit at the football field.

Wallace Maultsby, I believe it was, hid in the quilt bin and when Miss Daughtry reached in, he grabbed her hand. With such antics as these it's a wonder that the matrons stayed on, but whatever warfare there was between us was carried on in fun, not wantonly or maliciously. And, it never got out of control nor did it leave anyone hurt. The key to peaceful and successful living arose out of respect for the matron's authority and her ability to apply it even-handedly. To imagine two women serving as surrogate parents for thirty-five boys or girls suggests the impossibility of it but for the matron it became a way of life, a calling, a mission, a way of living out their faith. They had other choices: many had taught school prior to becoming matrons. There was also the love that developed between matron and child, perhaps the strongest bond of all.

Mary Cook, matron at the Fleming cottage for small girls, died in 1934. On her headstone was carved, "She loved children and children loved her." It was true. All the girls called her "Cookie." Hazel Owen came to the orphanage in 1930 and after one night with Mrs. Bannister was sent to the Fleming. Each evening the girls crowded around Cookie for devotions and to sing a song or two. Afterwards Cookie pulled forth her rule book and read off the rules. Who did so and so. The guilty ones raised hands. No one was allowed to tattle. Those guilty of simple naughtiness were not allowed to kiss Cookie goodnight. For pulling hair it was a gentle lick or two with a hairbrush. For serious stuff the sinner was made to stand in the corner, one hand over the mouth and the other on top of the head, and sometimes this was on one foot. This system of check and balance, of rewards and punishment, was carried on in each cottage and in modern parlance would be known as tough love. It was the rule of relationship, not only in the cottage, but on the farm, in the valley, at the print shop, sewing room, laundry. From it came respect of one for another.

Little acts made lasting expressions. One alumnus told me of being sick when he was at the Simmons and of Miss Ballard picking the seeds from raisins and feeding him. It was his first solid food as he recovered. He did not forget.

We expected more from our matrons than from anyone else. They were expected to have a measure of intelligence; intelligence of the common sense variety, wisdom of ordinary things, a knowledge of what's going on in the world. They were not mere housekeepers. To them we brought problems. From them we extracted suggestions to the solutions. They were not Latin or Greek scholars but they kept up with what was happening outside our boundaries and passed it to us for our own minds to assimilate and digest.

The matrons did not weep over our orphanhood nor pet us because of it nor exhibit the attitude that they were abandoning a life elsewhere for the sake of the poor orphan. They were not vessels of maudlin sentimentality, an attitude that instinctively causes either concealed or revealed contempt in a child. But, they were genuinely interested in us as persons, in our problems, our peculiarities, and our development. They brought to bear on our actions the empathy and understanding of an adult mind.

We tested wits against the matrons as against no other workers and, as noted, they were not pushovers. If caught in a misdeed we knew that punishment would follow, leading to another battle of wits as we plea bargained to get the sentence reduced. Did any good come from this? Sure, a sense of right and wrong, of cause and effect, of action and consequence. But, perhaps another; most orphanage boys became good husbands and the girls became good wives. They knew housework and dishwashing and sweeping yards — all from punishments decreed when misguided conduct was detected.

Mr. Neilson confessed that he never really understood just who the "workers" were. If a stranger were asked to address the "Workers' Council," an association that included every employee and met for pleasure as well as for business, he might be told by the school principal, "Come talk to the teachers and workers."

Mrs. Frazier and Miss Ballard would ask, "Can you speak to the matrons and workers?"

Mr. McKoin would say "The farm force and workers" and for Cy Howell it would be, "The print shop force and workers." Mr. Neilson spoke of "The Pastor and workers" and Miss Sallie "The office force and workers."

Collectively, the teachers, matrons, office staff — all employees — these were the workers and the distinction of place of service carried over to frequency of contact. Contacts with office staff were infrequent. Contact with Mr. Paul, for example, was inevitable for most every boy and girl. He served as farm foreman and superintendent of buildings and grounds and taught Sunday school forty-four years. His presence was evident in many phases of campus life and he was a man on whom nothing was lost. He bent an ear to the soil and raised an eye to the heavens to decide when the time was ripe to drop seed. He watched boys more assiduously for, as he said, "There's nothing else to make a man from."

Daily he gathered his men, six or seven, and his boys, twenty or thirty, grouped them as to task and place, instructed them as to team of mules, tractor, truck, or wagon and sent them forth. During the day he made his rounds to check on progress, now at this cottage, now at Roses field, Long field, Gold Hole, or Finch's, at the grainery, in the silos. He was the most controlled of men, never daunted by a task or mishap, never ruffled, never excited, always pleasant, always willing to take time with a boy.

One time Mr. Paul took more time with me than I wanted. John Anderson, J. D. Branch, and I were playing ball in a filled grain bin on the top floor of the grainery on a rainy afternoon. I threw the ball out the window and told J. D. to get it. When he reached ground John and I leaned out the window and pelted him with handfulls of wheat. Unknown to us, Mr. Paul was working on a tractor in a roofed but open basement workshop. He saw the grain raining down. "Who is that?" he asked J. D.

"Ted Chandler and John Anderson," J. D. answered.

"Tell them to come down," Mr. Paul instructed.

Without anger he gave us his pocket knife and told us to go cut some switches. We cut a half dozen or so from a nearby privet hedge. John stripped the leaves off. I looked them over. "They'll not do," I told John. "They're too big." I cut a half dozen more, thinner and left the leaves intact, to soften the blow. Without anger Mr. Paul switched away until they were all broken. We cried, but, honestly, it wasn't that bad, and the leaves did help. Years later I married Fran, Mr. Paul's youngest daughter, but in our many talks he never mentioned the switching.

Cy Howell, with Edgar Brock and Ted Hethcock, all former orphanage boys, ran the print shop. Cy loved a good joke and enjoyed pranks but his serious side constantly added to the honor of the orphanage. During the war he carefully compiled records of the brave men and women the orphanage sent into the service of the country and reminded the alumni constantly that they belonged to a group whose loyalty and courage shone splendidly in dark days. He stimulated our pride and contributed to our self-respect, a gift far greater than money.

Cy started the Alumni Notes column in the *Charity and Children,* laying before the Baptists of North Carolina the most convincing possible evidence that their money hadn't been wasted. His eager eye never overlooked a decent thing done by any former orphanage boy or girl; and the long record of fine things and fine people shown in his column proved beyond dispute that every dollar invested had yielded rich returns. So he added to our self-respect as well as to that of the Baptists.

When I was an intern at Baptist Hospital Cy suffered a massive heart attack that threw his heart into failure. He was admitted to the care of Dr. Emory Miller and I was the house doctor. He flirted with death for days and after months had only regained partial health. I visited him several times after he returned home.

171

It was always a blessing to be in his company as well as in the company of Mrs. Howell, who also grew up at the orphanage. As Mae Ammons she lived in Madison County before her orphanage days and, as this was the same county of our origin, we were able to trace family lines and claim a degree of kinship.

Cy's illness distressed thousands. They sent expressions of admiration and of love and ardent hopes for a swift recovery. He continued to compile records of alumni deeds but never regained good health. When he died the mantle of compiling alumni deeds passed to Franklin Bailey and now rests in the laps of Bill and Louise Sisk, both orphanage alumni.

Franklin Bailey had a run-in with Dr. Kesler, the General Manager before Mr. Greer, on the day of his arrival at the orphanage. Dr. Kesler's imposing and stern God-like demeanor struck fear into Frank and that fear did not abate until Dr. Kesler's accidental death when his car was hit by a train shortly before our arrival. But, Dr. Kesler was seen quite differently by Roland Cain. He wrote:

> In 1906 I was nearing my tenth birthday when I alighted from old No. 35 at Thomasville and was met at the station by Charlie Hanna and William Powell with old "Daisy" and the buggy. I was away from home for the first time, and had no idea in the world what was before me. I was not long in finding out — and I shall always look back upon those seven years as the happiest years of my life.
>
> It was probably several days after I arrived at Thomasville before I saw Dr. Kesler. My first sight of him was early one morning in a heavy downpour of rain. I looked out of the Mother's Building window and I saw a man with an umbrella in one hand and a shovel in the other. He was digging dirt and trash out of the drain ditch along the side of the road, where it was clogged up and causing the water to overflow across the road and washing it badly. That was my first sight of Dr. Kesler, and to me it will always remain typical of the man.
>
> I saw him on many other occasions doing such jobs

as that — setting an example worthy of emulation. I would like to relate some of them, but time and space will not permit, for each one would be a sermon within itself.

As a little fellow at the Orphanage, I stood in absolute awe of Dr. Kesler. There was something about the man which overwhelmed me. He seemed to be so rock-like, so strong, so unshakable, so unbending, and shall I say, so king-like. His word to me, was indisputable fact, and it never occurred to me to question it.

He was indeed a true friend of the orphan. If he had any visible fault, it was evidenced only in his rock-like qualities which made it somewhat difficult for one of the little fellows at the Orphanage to approach him. This, of course, was in our imagination, for as I grew older, I found him to be kind and sympathetic and understanding, always ready and willing to help in any way he could.

When I finished the school at the Orphanage, it was necessary for me to take a year at a preparatory school before I could enter college. The Orphanage had only nine grades at the time — not sufficient to enter college. I worked a year and saved almost enough money to see me through the necessary year of prep school. However, just before the end of the year I saw that I was going to be $50.00 short. I wrote to Dr. Kesler, and immediately a check for $50 with a note for the same amount was forthcoming. I signed the note and returned it to him, and was thus enabled to finish out the year. When, after two years in College and two years in the Army, and another year spent in working, I sent him a check for the loan repayment, he wrote me a nice letter, the memory of which I still cherish.

Several years later, when I was graduating from Law School, I sent Dr. Kesler an invitation to the commencement exercises. I received a brief letter from him, in which he said: "I knew what was in the envelope even before I opened it. I always knew that some day you would do it." Such words of encouragement and expressions of confidence in the old graduates, were typical of Dr. Kesler.

As I grow older, I cherish more and more the seven years of my contact and acquaintance with Dr. Kesler. In those seven years I felt the whip-lash of his tongue, when I breached the rules of discipline. I even felt the "rod" one time held in his strong right hand for a more serious breach of discipline. I "know" how firm he was — and I cherish his memory for it. His imprint is left indelibly upon my life, and I feel that I am better fitted for life, because of my association with Dr. Kesler.

As viewed by one from down "underneath" Dr. Kesler reminded me of the high mountain peak, with its great granite boulders supporting it. It seemed that his face reflected the glory of the sunlight, no matter what storms and clouds were gathered around his feet. There is no doubt in my mind but what he stood out a full head and shoulders above the crowds. He was a man with a purpose in life. He permitted nothing to stand in the way of that purpose, and because of this I know there are hundreds of old graduates of the Baptist Orphanage of North Carolina who are made stronger. I know that there are thousands of people in North Carolina who have been made better and happier because of the life of this man.

Yes, within the view of one down underneath, his memory still lives. His life still reflects the glories of the evening sun light. His influence will linger throughout the lives of hundreds who are now living — and I know the world has been made better by the life of Dr. Martin Luther Kesler — A Doctor of Humanities.

Fair are the meadows, fairer still the woodlands,
Robed in the blooming garb of spring;
Jesus is fairer, Jesus is purer,
Who makes the woeful heart to sing.

Such words epitomize Dr. Kesler. He saw beauty in each life and in each plant, and with discerning eye, intellectual and moral power, and muscle, he worked at flowering the campus and

174

shaping the child, doing both in shirtsleeves with vigor.

Mr. Greer, a history professor, entered the world of children and straightway became one of us. George Bailey was sent to him with a note explaining George's errant behavior. The matron asked, "Would you please punish accordingly." Mr. Greer invited George into his study and asked if he knew how to play Chinese checkers. "I have never been able to beat my sons at this game," he told George.

"George said, "Sure, I know how to play." He coached Mr. Greer on winning tactics for an hour and then returned to cottage bearing in hand the countersigned note.

Mr. Greer came upon Mace Brown crying at the foot of one of the giant campus oaks and, taking him in hand, suggested that they take a ride. He placed Mace in a wheelbarrow and toured the campus, pointing out interesting places of promise.

Mr. Roosevelt, called to lead the Nation at the time that Mr. Greer was called to lead us, said:

> Happiness lies not in the mere possession of money; it lies in the joy of achievement, in the thrill of creative effort. The joy and moral stimulation of work no longer must be forgotten in the mad chase of evanescent profits. These dark days will be worth all they cost us if they teach us that our true destiny is not to be ministered unto but to minister to ourselves and to our fellow-men.
>
> Recognition of the falsity of material wealth as the standard of success goes hand in hand with the abandonment of the false belief that public office and high political position are to be valued only by the standards of pride of place and personal profit; and there must be an end to a conduct in banking and in business which too often has given to a sacred trust the likeness of callous and selfish wrongdoing.
>
> Small wonder that confidence languishes, for it thrives only on honesty, on honor, on the sacredness of obligations, on faithful protection, on unselfish performance; without them it can not live.

Near the same time John Dillinger's father, seventy-three years old, rode in the hearse to pick up his boy's body, gunned down by the F.B.I. He said, "I never upheld John. He might have been a citizen if his mother hadn't died when he was a little boy."

It was Mr. Greer's view that every one of his orphans should be upheld. He was determined that none should land in prison. "Every child," he said, "has the right to excel. For some, marbles are fine. Try to be the best marble shooter, the best speller, first in your class in school, the first to outrun the others, the first to milk your cows. The girls should excel in some part of their work or in some part of the curriculum. If not, then the curriculum should be broadened." He believed that the boy or girl who could be led to be first in some legitimate thing would never end up in an illegitimate undertaking. "Every child," he said "has the right to special notice and what's more, he or she will have it."

Mr. Greer and the other workers were convinced that our orphanage was the best in the world and strove continually to enlist people in the great undertaking for their own good. "Our children are a blessing, not a burden," he said. He considered us weapons in a battle to keep people from being consumed with selfishness. "These children will keep your hearts tender and kind," he told church congregations, "You are asked to sacrifice for them, but it doesn't compare with the sacrifice they have made in order to help you."

Mr. Greer won the hearts of all during his first days as General Manager by calling everyone to a get-together in the auditorium. There we clapped and cheered and whistled as he sang his way through a portion of his repertoire of Appalachian ballads and, tall and dignified looking, danced around in a soft shoe routine as Mrs. Greer played the dulcimer. With vigor he sang tales of romance and adventure; "I've got a gal in Sourwood Mountain," "Black Jack Joe," "The Golden Willowtree," "Granny has left to you her old Arm Chair," "The Fella Thatta Looks Like Me." From that time we were his; here was one in whom there was no guile, no deceit, another in whom we could trust.

176

When I became a medical student at Chapel Hill Mr. Greer sent word to join him at supper. He had left the General Manager's post but remained on the Board of Trustees. I visited him and later as a fatal illness began invading he quizzed me about his condition. Dr. John Sessions, one of my mentors at the medical school, was his physician.

"Do you believe," Mr. Greer would begin, "That the diagnosis I have been given is correct?" Imagine, pitting me against one of my professors, as though my opinion had worth. None the less, I spilled out my opinion without benefit of experience, not once understanding that his purpose was to boost mine. It did that.

Mr. Greer's success, just as the success of each General Manager before him, was a combination of unswerving dedication, vision of immense proportions, and good people who tended to stay on the job for periods measured in decades, not in mere years. Miss Sallie served 73 years, Mr. Paul, 44 years, Miss Turner, 39, Archibald Johnson, 39, and Miss Hattie, 34 years, Doc Early, about 35 years, Miss Council, Miss Ethel Johnson, and Miss Myra Olive, over 20 years each. There were others, many others, whose exact years of service are unknown to me.

Mr. Greer was ambassador and orator, Miss Eulalia Turner worked her miracles out of the public eye. She counted dresses and shirts, pillowcases, quilts, jars of peaches, loads of apples; making certain we would not starve, die of exposure or appear too ragged in dress. She insisted on the shapeless bathing suit that covered everything but, as well, decreed that out of the swimming pool the orphanage look be not one of identical or uniform garb.

Miss Sallie and I, during the years we ran close tilt, had minds magnetized to opposite poles, but even in the midst of our war I had some appreciation of her mind's range. She had an interest in everything, on every continent and added new words and assimilated new facts at a dizzying pace. Do you know where Liverno, Italy is?, What is the South American drink, mate, made from?. On and on it ranged.

In her quiet way she also influenced many lives. She loaned

Adlai Stevenson money to go to college; he secured the loan with an insurance policy.

In October, 1915, Adlai, then principal of the Robbinsville High School, wrote Dr. Kesler:

Dear Dr. Kesler:
I guess you will be surprised to get this letter, but I want to lay before you a matter of my heart. It has been burning in me for a long time, but I have resisted it. I am going to preach — and just as soon as I get fully straightened out, I am going to some foreign field. My first duty is to God. I want you to pray for me daily. I know how weak and sinful I am but I am determined to let him have his way.

I am getting along nicely with my school work. O, we need more strong men to learn and live in the hills. There are five churches right around me without a pastor.

Please write me when you can.
Sincerely,
Adlai Stevenson

In October 1918 Miss Sallie received the following telegram:

Miss Sallie McCracken:
Deeply regret to inform you that Sergeant Adlai Stevenson, machine gun battalion, is officially reported killed in action September 27.
Signed,
Harris, Adj. Gen.

The wire was followed by a letter from Captain Oscar Mills, Co. D, 115 Machine Gun Company:

Sgt. Stevenson was killed near Roisel, France, September 27, 1918, about 3 P.M. and was buried at Lincourt, France, September 28....Sgt. Stevenson was an excellent soldier and a fine young man. He was rec-ommended for a commission and at the time he was killed, was preparing to leave for the officers training school.

Miss Sallie was paid Adlai's insurance and invested it. Years later she used the money to light the steeple of our church, to place chimes on the Baptist church in Sendai, Japan, and to light the steeple of Wake Forest University's Wait Chapel.

The Mills Home Church elected Miss Sallie and Miss Turner to their Board of Deacons and for years Miss Sallie chaired the group, alternating with Mr. Paul. Miss Sallie remained at the orphanage until her death, 47 days short of being 100 years old. She had invested wisely and left a sizable estate to the orphanage.

There were a hundred faces to the lives of the workers. No one of us knew them all. But, of them we can be grateful for a certain gift. It was the gift of belief in ourselves. They dignified our lives by their friendship and by giving the gifts of love and belief. Had it not been this way, we and they together for this span of time, how differently life would have been for each of us. As it is it did not happen the other way, the unthinkable way.

Some of Our Workers
Front row: Mr. Ellis, Mr. Hughes, Mr. Louya, Mr. Paul, Mr. Richardson. Back row: Frank Bailey, Bill Sisk, Mr. Raper.

179

Miss Hester and her boys. Ted is fifth from the right on the back row.

Mr. Paul and his friends.

14

Expressions

As we prepared to depart the orphanage we expressed our understanding and appreciation of it.

An orphanage boy wrote:

I came to the Orphanage after my father died. My mother was to find a way to care for a family of five. After a year or so she sent my two oldest brothers to Jackson. We had it a little easier after that, but it was still hard for her to send the three who were left to school. My mother heard of the Baptist Orphanage, so she made arrangements for us to be cared for there. When I first came here I knew I would like it very much. Although I have had several misunderstandings since I have been here, I think it is a swell place.

My education has been provided for very splendidly. If I had not entered the Orphanage, I, like many others, would be uneducated. The Orphanage has provided for me eleven great years in school with very fine teachers. I, being the only one of my family to graduate, am very grateful for this help in school.

An orphanage girl wrote:

When visitors come to the Orphanage, so often they ask the girls and boys these questions:

"How long have you been here?" "Are you happy in this home?" "What are going to do when you leave Mills Home?" Then, judging by facial expressions, there is one more they would like to ask, but they dare not, "Why are you here?"

Some of these questions I shall answer now.

About fourteen years ago my father was shot and killed by a Negro. At that time my mother was ill, and only a few days after my father's death, she died also, leaving nine children without father or mother. From that time until two years later, I lived with my grandmother, and then the death-angel entered our home again and took her.

I then was left with no place to go, and no one to care for me as a mother and father would. I was put in a boarding school until a place was opened up. Soon I found that I was to be sent to the Baptist Orphanage. Of course I didn't want to come, because parting with my old friends was hard for me. They told me that I would find many friends, and they would be to me as brothers and sisters. I hardly thought that could be possible. But one cold day in October, 1936, when I was nine years of age, I entered the arch of a most beautiful campus. Yes, I missed my sisters and old friends, but in a short while I found many new ones who made up in a fine way for the loss of the old ones.

My first days at the Orphanage were spent at the infirmary. These were not pleasant days. I was homesick, moody and resentful. For illustration, the pastor came to see me. He asked me my name. My answer makes me hang my head in shame. I told him it was none of his business. My appreciation of the pastor is so great that I can not even express it.

182

The Orphanage has done more for me than I could have asked for. Had I not come to Mills Home, I often wonder where I would be and what I would be. To me Mills Home means most everything. We are trained in many things and are given the best of attention here.

We have a well-graded school of which Mr. Romulus Skaggs is the principal. The faculty is made up of fourteen members. Since entering high school I have had the advantages offered by these departments, literary, home economics, commercial, musical, and athletics. Of all the activities on the campus I like sports and music best. I am a member of the choir and also active on the basketball team.

We are trained not only mentally and physically but spiritually as well. The boys and girls have the advantages of training offered in the following organizations: the church, the Sunday school, the B. T. U., and the young peoples' organizations of the W. M. U. All of these have meant something to my life. I joined the church when I was twelve years old and have been a member of these organizations since that time.

To the workers at Mills Home and to the Baptists of North Carolina who have made it possible for me to have this training and this home, I want to say, "Thank you."

An orphanage boy wrote:

I was born June 25, 1921. I don't know what happened or what kind of day it was except that I was born. But I love to think that it was a beautiful June day — flowers blooming, cool mountain breezes blowing, and a nice peaceful place. It must have been like that because it was in the mountains, in a peaceful little town. The houses are miles apart, and my home was in a beautiful spot. There was plenty of room to breathe and a beautiful view of the mountains and valleys below. We lived near a small town and I lived out in the country. The community was very much like the little village of Sweet Auburn in

183

Goldsmith's *Deserted Village.*

It was in this little village that I spent the early years of my life — climbing mountains, hunting with my sling shot, going fishing, and doing everything that is natural for any boy to do. I remember my first day at school. I was scared pink. Even to look at the little one-room-school-house — for that is where I first went to school — made me shudder. I wanted to run away into the hills where I could spend the day picking blackberries and where I would be safe.

These were happy days and I was contented. But when I was about seven years old, my father died, leaving my mother and twelve children all alone. There were six boys and six girls in the family. It became so hard on my mother that she soon died too. The three oldest boys were able to work and help out, but I'm afraid I was only in the way. We had to do something, because there were so many of us. They finally made arrangements for six of us — the six youngest — to come to the Baptist orphanage. I was one of the six.

I hated to leave all my friends and my happy life there, but I knew that it was best for me if I ever wanted to be somebody. I wanted to become a gentleman and so I didn't mind so much.

I loved Mills Home from the very start. I was a little hesitant at first, when I saw all those thirty-five boys with blue shirts and khaki pants on crowding around and inspecting me. But they seemed to like me very well and I was soon one of the number. This was at the Simmons Nursery, and my first duty was the house. I learned to sweep and make beds and wash windows. I worked in the house and kitchen until I was about ten years old. Then I worked on the farm for a year — picking beans and carrying water to the boys driving the tractor. When I was about twelve I began working in the school as office boy. During this same year I became a Christian and was baptized. To me this was a very important year in my life; I seemed to learn more that year than any other. I got a new start in life.

At the age of fourteen I entered high school and started working in the print shop. I liked to work there because it was so new to me. There were many machines running and so much going on. I liked the linotype best, because it could do so much more than the others. I had to wash off presses and sweep floors at first, though; but in a few years I was running the linotype.

When I first entered high school, I began to wonder what I wanted to do. What was my ambition? I began to think what I could do and what I wanted to do. I wanted to be an actor! It didn't come to me all of a sudden like that; the stage had always appealed to me. And I had always wanted to be an actor. This was when we gave a big play every year, and I always longed to be in it. I would imagine myself as a great actor doing my very best. It was so much fun pretending I was someone else and acting like him. I found it very easy to do. Yes, my first year in high school I decided I would be an actor on the stage. And it's that I shall be if I have the talent. I think it is a very worthy ambition. I have prayed to God and asked him about it. And there has come a feeling in my heart that I should be an actor. Many times I have caught myself just sitting and thinking how I would ever be one. I want to go to school and study dramatics. I would like it very much and it is perhaps the best thing.

I am now a senior in high school. I am seventeen years old. In a few more days I shall have to leave Mills Home and start out in the world to achieve my ambition. Mills Home shall ever be dear to me, as the only home I ever knew. It was here that I found my ambition — my longing for the stage.

Through the study of Shakespeare's plays I found a deeper interest in the stage. He is my favorite writer. I have read many of his plays and studied them. To me he is the greatest writer that ever lived.

"All the world's a stage,
And all the men and women merely players.
They have their exits and their entrances,
And one man in his time plays many parts."

An orphanage girl wrote:

I suppose, as you read this, that you have these things in mind: What tragedy caused her to enter the Orphanage? How long has she been there? What has she accomplished during her nine year's stay there?

Before coming to the Orphanage, I lived happily with my father, mother, and eleven brothers and sisters. One day my father and mother went to town to do some shopping. The seven of my oldest brothers and sisters were away from home too. The four younger ones were left at home, I being one of them. We were playing happily in the yard when we heard a loud crash. We stopped our play and curiously watched the train which had wrecked a car. While we were trying to figure out what it was all about, a little negro girl came up and said, "I'm powerful sorry, but you all's ma and pa just got kilt in a train wreck."

My other brothers and sisters were summoned home at once. As we tried to plan for the future, no one knew what to do; for none of us had ever worked away from home. Something had to be done! Our house was a rented one and we had to give it up, unless we found some way to pay the rent.

Finally one of my daddy's brothers offered a solution. He had already gotten in touch with the Baptist Orphanage at Thomasville and the three youngest of us were accepted into its fold.

When we were told this, we cried as though our hearts would break, because we had visions of harsh, misunderstanding people who, if you dared speak one word out loud, would surely slap you down. But to my surprise, everything was the very opposite from what we had expected. I had no experiences which would have aided me

186

in my future life. Now as you read this, I want all of you to know that I have been trained for many things, things such as: learning to cook, sew and clean house. I have had an education, both in school and church life, given to me by one of the finest teachers in North Carolina. When I get sick, I am well cared for. We have a well equipped library that fills every need a reader could expect.

All of these I have because of you. I want to say "thank you" with all my heart.

An orphanage boy wrote:

In February, 1935, my mother died. Three months later my father died also. That is the primary reason for my coming to the orphanage. However, that is not the only reason. My guardians came to the decision that it would be best for me to come here and receive the training I might not have otherwise received.

I am today in good health — better, I know, than I would be if I were on the outside. We have a good doctor, and a trained nurse to care for the sick. When a serious case appears, the patient is taken to High Point or Winston-Salem to be ministered to.

In the sports field we are fortunate in having nearly all kinds typical in this part of the country. We have quite a few cups and medals which are now in our library.

I am glad I came here if an education were the only thing I received. One has many opportunities here to receive more variety in education than at any other one place in the world. That is my opinion, and I am sure that I would be backed up by many other boys and girls in or out of the home.

Here at the Orphanage we are also taught to be sociable to everyone. You will find nearly all of the larger boys and girls here able to speak to or be with any person, no matter what class they may be in. We have the privilege very often of hearing famous people speak and that, too, helps in our social life.

We have an opportunity that perhaps boys and girls on the outside do not have, and that is, we are trained to do many things. The boys work at the farm, poultry yard, dairy, print shop, painting, plumbing, carpenter shop and many other things. The girls work at the laundry, sewing room, hospital, and kitchen. You see, there is a great variety in our work.

In the spiritual life here we have the privilege of attending at will, or being a member of: the church, Sunday school, the choir, B. T. U., G. A., R. A., Y. W. A., and Sunbeams. You will find all the boys and girls attending nearly all of these activities. Seldom does a boy or girl graduate from here without being baptized. We have a very fine pastor.

Now, I am ready to face the future with whatever hardships it may offer, better than I would be if I had not come here.

The present struggle between nations is going to do a lot in deciding my future. If I see I am not going to play a part in ending this struggle, I am going to attend college if it is at all possible. After I leave this beloved home and until death I will always carry with me the teaching and training I received at the Orphanage.

An orphanage girl wrote:
I was born in the year 1920 in a small village. Only four years of my life were spent in this neighborly village.

Due to my father's death, I was transmitted into a new home; a home for many hundreds of boys and girls who could not be provided for elsewhere. Luck certainly came my way when I was placed in such a home as this. Of course I realize it now, but when I first came, I thought I was having the worst luck of anybody living. I was very unhappy and homesick. I longed to be where my mother was. I often cried when I missed the presence of my mother and father. Although I knew my father was dead, I couldn't bear the thought of having him taken away from me. On top of that, I was taken away from my dear mother. I know I was a great deal of trouble to my mother, (as I have been told), but of course I didn't know any better then. Mother had to work extra hard to keep up a family of four after my father died, so naturally she had to have the help of someone.

Miss Hattie Edwards, from the Baptist Orphanage of North Carolina, came to her aid just in time. My mother hated to part with us, but she knew it was all for the best.

When I came to the Orphanage, everyone tried to cheer me up, but I felt like no one could ever replace my mother's love. I know now that I had merely gone through what every boy and girl that comes here has to go through.

As the years have passed, I have become aware of my environment. I have been living with a large group of boys and girls for fifteen years and have learned to think of them as my own brothers and sisters. Although Mills Home is well known to the public to be an institution, it is to me a real home and it will always be an "ideal home" for boys and girls. Everyone has wonderful opportunities here, and since we are taught to realize the importance of the various activities, we make the most of what is offered us. Every boy and girl is trained in such a way that he or she will be fitted to further develop a worthy profession when he graduates.

I have had the privilege of living in every girl's cottage on the campus with the exception of the Whitty Building. I have received training in various ways from these many different matrons that will remain with me as I grow older because I have realized the value of it and appreciate it.

Back in my earlier days when I couldn't understand every problem I often grew tired of the place in which I was living. Times were getting wearisome also for my mother about this time and she felt the need of me to come live with her. Worry after worry fell upon me. I hardly knew what to do. I was discouraged in every way.

189

I had no one in whom to confide because everything was beyond my explaining. I didn't have a special reason for wanting to leave, but I thought I could be happier with my mother since she wanted me to come. Although I was told about the mistake I was making, I took no second thought from that angle, and so I went to live with her.

I was very happy and pleased for a while, but as time passed, I grew very miserable of my environment. People were not at all like they were at Mills Home. I would often recall outstanding moments of my life at Mills Home and I wished more and more I were back there to enjoy life with my friends. As many times as I have felt the need of prayer, I have never sensed the need so badly in my life as I did then. This experience has taught me a great lesson. It has also given me a different and broader outlook on life.

I stayed with Mother only three months and was back at Mills Home before school started in the fall. How the authorities there even considered taking me back, God only knows, because I felt as if I didn't deserve it. I hesitated to go back because I did not feel worthy of the offer, but I know that all people make mistakes, but if given another chance and profits by their mistakes, they will have nothing to be ashamed of. I was determined to make my life count and prove myself worthy of my support. I was very happy indeed to be back and also very grateful.

Since I have been back at Mills Home, I have found more importance in the various activities than ever before. I grasped opportunities that were offered me with a more determined attitude to make them count.

Although sport life is a great asset on the campus, I couldn't participate in every one and make room for other things. I thoroughly enjoy them just the same and always will. When I had the choice of basketball or music, I gladly took music, realizing it would do me more good in the future. Although sportsmanship is practiced and developed in the realm of athletics, it also has its place in music.

Music helps one to develop his moral attitudes and it also strengthens character. I have been singing in the glee club, choir and trio for a number of years, but not until Mr. W. B. Lord took up the training of me in these various organizations for the past three years did I really know how to appreciate good music. Mr. Lord has meant a lot to me because he has offered what I have desired for many years. I took piano under Mrs. Lord and feel the same towards her.

I have found a real purpose in music and that is to help me to appreciate and enjoy the finer and more cultural things in life and to develop my moral standards. After all, as the saying goes, "Purpose is what gives life a meaning." Music plays a large part in the making of a well-rounded person.

I realize that I have a future before me and that I must face it very sincerely; therefore, I must plan ahead. My greatest desire in life is to be an excellent home-maker, and my ambition, if I can carry it out, is to become a Home-Economics teacher. I choose this profession because it teaches everything a woman should know in order to make a good home, and I am sure every normal girl is looking forward to having a home of her own some day.

The duties I have had while at Mills Home are good fundamentals for this type of work. In taking up this work besides learning for myself what life holds for me, I feel as if I can help many other people who need to realize their responsibilities in life also.

Although I took a commercial course in high school instead of a foreign language, I feel that it will do me more good in the future. I want to go to a junior college in order to secure the subjects necessary for a more advanced training in Home Economics. The commercial course and the music I have taken including other subjects, will serve as my electives in college.

There is no work worthwhile and well performed without effort; therefore, it makes no difference how much hard work it takes to do this work. As long as I can work, hope and live for my ambition to bring me a real success, I will willingly and proudly look to my foundation, "The Mills Home Baptist Orphanage." I know I will be the happiest person in the world, knowing that I have made my life what I had so long desired, and accomplished what was before me. "Life is good; success is possible for all but the lazy. What is there to fear. We must know that we have quite enough skill to do some work well; then we must find work and do it."

15

War

The last days of my childhood were also the last days of the orphanage as we knew it. It was to go on, of course, and in the forefront as before, but protagonists of darkness were changing the world and we were to witness global machinations as well as local inevitabilities.

The exodus of big boys was not to begin until after war was declared but before that day we were well represented on the high seas especially and less well in Army and Marine enclaves. Ralph Duncan was on the Yorktown and when it went down he survived. His brother Ed was in the Marines. Harold Haynie, and George, Frank, and Nelson Bailey were pulling destroyer duty in the North Atlantic on the USS Roe. Fat Greene was aboard the Jacob Jones and J. R. Dotson was on the USS Seattle. Grover Bradshaw was aboard the Owl and Luther Whetstine was in service school. Richard Mitchell, Judy Woods, and James Allen VanLandingham were also in the Navy.

Brother John graduated at the head of the class of 1941 in May. His thirty five classmates comprised the largest class to ever graduate from the orphanage school. He remained on campus, continuing to run the linotype for Cy Howell. In September he enrolled at Mars Hill College.

Cal continued to operate the other linotype machine and during late summer went to Danville, Virginia, as a delegate to the annual meeting of school representatives of orphanages. He, Oma Shoe, Clara Hicks, Gertie Patterson, and Bill and Bob Tate argued problems of orphanage life with representatives from the Presbyterian orphanage, the Elon College Home, The Children's Home of Winston-Salem, and Junior Order Home. They summarized their deliberations and submitted recommendations to the management.

As for me, I was still reading. Miss Council ran her usual reading contest at the library, offering a prize for those who read twelve books, and answered fourteen questions such as; "What is a pseudonym?" "Mark Twain is the pseudonym for _____?," "What queer character charged a windmill?," "Who was arrested for stealing a loaf of bread?." An additional prize was offered for the best essay on "Treasures Found in Books." During the summer I read *Les Miserables* and suffered eye strain, causing my head to ache even more.

December 7, 1941, was a clear crisp day with the silvery blue and white skies peculiar to pre-winter days. It had rained on Thursday, settling the smoky haze and leaving the atmosphere clean and fresh. Sunday school was taught as usual but church was held in a hushed breath, for the crisis with Japan loomed large. We met for worship in subdued hope. Many of our workers and children had joined with other church members in town the week before in an all night prayer vigil for peace.

I had transferred to the Watson Cottage in June and on December 7, at the first report of Pearl Harbor, was preparing to go to the barn for the afternoon milking. The report of the bombing came over the radio in the midst of a music program. In Winston-Salem a choral group was rendering Handel's Messiah at the Centenary Methodist Church and the announcer broke in during the solo, "Comfort Ye My People." The remainder of the oratorio went unbroadcast if not unsung.

194

The destruction of life, aircraft, and seapower at Pearl Harbor threw us into the business of war. The big boys saw the end of life as they knew it and gradually and calmly began signing up to fight injustice, persecution, exploitation, oppression, and especially tyrannical aims to subjugate the world.

We had hardly begun when the harsh reality of war struck. In February Fat Greene was declared lost at sea when the Jacob Jones was sunk by a German U Boat in the North Atlantic. His death was the first of eleven and the whole campus was saddened, for he was very popular.

Because of the war the radio became a sort of omniscient presence. It was not a cabinet, a jumble of tubes and electrical phenomena, or a man in the studio; it attained a godlike hereness.

"What does the radio say?," we asked solemnly. The radio said this, the radio warned against that; the radio instructed, urged, uplifted, directed, admonished, foretold, exhorted, and expanded and, even in the face of war, still entertained.

The trains continued to pass the orphanage in uncounted numbers day and night, their mission now outweighing their nuisance value. They continued to interrupt sleep, disturbed the radio, stifled conversation, but now they were more than a reminder and symbol of the war, they were a tangible part of war itself.

Uniformed men and women in pullman cars and armaments on flat cars carried away threads of conversation as our thoughts traveled on down the track with the soldiers, guns, and tanks.

At train stations Life magazine captured wartime drama by photographing countless leavetakings between couples too absorbed in each other to know or care who saw.

The mystique of the man in uniform carried to popular songs; girls were encouraged to "Don't Say No to a Soldier." This caused Mr. McMillan to warn our girls that a scoundrel, a dastard, a reprobate in uniform was still a scoundrel, dastard, or reprobate. Mr. Greer actually had a misbehaving sailor — not an orphanage boy — thrown off campus. He drew the ire of the swabby's chief petty officer who wrote, "Sir, you cannot forbid your grounds to one dressed in a U. S. uniform."

195

Mr. Greer replied to the officer, "We do not tolerate such behavior as your man exhibited. Should he set foot here again we will have him locked up, even if he is draped in the U. S. flag."

The fabric of our days, a patchwork whose pattern we did not fully appreciate was still found to be pleasing and worthwhile.

Cal's class, the class of 1942, put on "The Absent-Minded Professor" as senior play. The fact that Cal wasn't in it most likely had nothing to do with its considerable success; it played to a packed house each of two performances. Following the graduation festivities and rituals the class of 1942 gathered their new clothes, drew the remains of their senior pay, packed their trunks and headed out to jobs, school, and the armed services.

Cal took a job as linotype operator with a newspaper in Mount Holly. As he left I moved up, a sophomore in high school. In the fall Cal enrolled at Mars Hill where John was beginning his second year.

At Christmas Cal and John returned to visit me, to get their Christmas bags, and for John to direct a Sunday evening program on the merits of attending college. He moderated a panel comprised of Bill Tate, Lois Edinger, Virginia Duncan, and Faye Rhinehart; students all at Mars Hill, except Lois who attended Meredith. The panel discussed the religious, social, and athletic life on college campuses.

On our campus the pigeons of the Downing cottage continued to circle as a cloud, settling to perch along a topmost ridge, a quaint and humorous crowd. Unperturbed for a moment, they were off again, swooping, gliding, perhaps disturbed by the airplanes. There were more planes than ever and they flew lower.

Mr. Galey and his boys continued to cut the grass with power mowers, making quite a fuss. Through the noise of the mowers and that of the planes overhead, crying continued to be heard; the newly arrived-four-year old overcome with homesickness, or the seasoned-seven-year old with a stubbed toe.

Coach Kearns enrolled fifty or so for the Fourth of July swimming contest but those exhorting us to beauty of form or swiftness of passage were mostly our own; excursions had come to an end. All trains were filled with troops.

Uptown, Mr. R. L. Pope, the mayor, called a town meeting to organize for total defense. The chief of police was empowered to deal with lawlessness. That, of course, was his job before the war, but now a committee helped him draft plans to assure the continuance of power, water, and the working of manufactories, even in the face of invasion. A local physician was charged to plan for evacuating and treating large numbers of casualties. The fire chief drafted volunteer firemen. A raucous horn with voice powerful enough to carry to the county line was mounted on City Hall.

In celebration of untested preparations the orphanage band led a victory parade through city streets. Next in line was our bus, filled with fifty little boys and girls waving small American flags from open windows.

We practiced blackouts in preparation for night-time bombing raids; grabbing quilts to blind glaring windows at the sounding of the raucous horn. The raid exercises usually ended about 9:30 but that mattered little, by that time we had been in bed at least half an hour. Louise McMillan in her column, Patchwork, in *Charity and Children*, wrote of her experiences during two blackout practices:

> We had our first blackout last April, a district blackout covering several counties. In my imagination I had pictured our family in a solemn huddle listening to the hideous noise of the siren, and bolstering our courage by thinking of all the brave people who had lived through actual air raids. But here came the first discrepancy between the dream and the reality.
>
> When the siren actually sounded I did not even hear it. Along with a large number of students and guests, I was attending the annual junior-senior banquet of the Mills Home High School, and the sound of music inside the gymnasium all but drowned out the air raid signal outside.
>
> It had been thought that the banquet would be over before the blackout began, but since the siren caught us in the gymnasium, we had to stay there until the all clear sounded. Someone extinguished the lights, the program

197

continued in darkness, and we spent out first blackout listening to an imperturbable junior deliver a dramatic recitation about the Irish.

Her performance was admirable, but I am afraid my mind wandered a little. I kept worrying about mother being at home by herself — if she has ever been afraid of anything, I don't know when it was — and wondering if she'd remember to put a blanket over the radio to keep the light from being visible. She says we never give her credit for having any intelligence. Well, anyway, it was all very different from what I had imagined.

And so it was with the blackout the other night. I will say that it was a success to the extent of showing up the vulnerability of our defenses.

This time, mother and I were at home by ourselves. In the afternoon we went to a great deal of pains to make my room light-proof, it being the easiest to blackout because of the size and position of the windows. After all our trouble, however, we realized that of all the rooms in the house it was probably the least safe in the event of a real raid. A corner room, unprotected by a porch outside, an upper story or even an attic, it constituted a fine example of the kind of place not to be in during an air raid. Even so, we decided to let it suffice for this time and make other arrangements later.

The second error we made was in regard to the living room fire. We shivered through the earlier part of the evening in order to keep as small a fire as possible, but when the siren blew there was a sizable bed of red hot coals in the grate. It wouldn't have mattered so much if there had not been seven large windows in our two connecting front rooms, none of which was shaded. Though we did our best with a fire screen, card table and what not, scrambling around frantically in the semi-darkness. The obstinate coal rallied its last dying forces and shuddered into flame.

I suppose we should have put out the fire with water,

but this was, after all, only a test. We readjusted the screens, hoping fervently that the table wouldn't catch fire, went out on the porch to see how much light was visible from without — *and straightway proceeded to lock ourselves out!*

It has been said that a thief can always find one window unlocked; so can mother. After floundering around in the darkness for a while, trying first one lock and then the other, she climbed in through a dining room window, with the unsteady aid of a rocker pushed up against the house, and thus opened the door from the inside.

By that time we had had quite enough of cold and darkness. We scuttled back to my room, a close, smothery retreat, smelling strongly of the camphor balls in which the blackout blankets had been packed. It was with untold relief that we heard the all-clear some minutes later.

The boy scouts mounted a drive to collect cooking fats, two boys each lugging five gallon cans down Johnsontown road, knocking on every door and asking for their excess grease. We thanked people, poured up until the large cans were filled and carried them to prearranged stations to await Coach Kearns in the orphanage truck.

We scouted orphanage lands, searching grown over spots behind barns, sheds, and the grainery and collected 15,000 pounds of burned out boilers, scrap metal, and junked machines. In Sunday school we were urged, after placing the tithe in the offering plate, to convert spare cash to defense stamps.

Orphanage boys were signing up at a rapid rate; those slated for graduation, if of age, were sorely tempted to have Mr. Greer sign to release them and many did. North Carolinians at large were being rejected for mental or physical inadequacies at the rate of 58%. Orphanage boys had a rejection rate of 1.4%. John persisted in efforts to enlist in the army but he was turned down because of too high arches of his feet. He finished at Mars Hill and moved on to Wake Forest to continue his studies. Cal finished one year at Mars Hill and joined the Navy. He was sent to Bainbridge, Maryland, for boot training and radio school.

The remoteness of the struggle was made immediate by the appearance of boys in uniform on campus and by their introduction of new lands by name: Tunisia, Sicily, Norfolk, New Guinea, Parris Island, San Diego, The Aleutians, New Brittain, Truk Island, Guam, Gilbert Island, Guadalcanal.

The orphanage newspaper was sent to every service man whose address was known. Louise McMillan caught the orphanage contingent up on the news by writing Alex Ross:

The Mills Home
Thomasville, North Carolina
October 30, 1942

Ensign J. A. Ross, Jr.
B. O. O. 800
Naval Air Station
Jacksonville, Fla.

Dear Alex:

As you probably know, a large number of old orphanage boys — in the case "old" means "former" and does not refer to age — are now serving in the armed forces of our country. Though we are trying to keep in touch with as many of them as possible, I am afraid that our list of addresses is far from complete. So if you know the location of an old boy who has not heard from any of us here at home, we'd appreciate your writing us about him.

In order that none should be left out among those whose addresses we do have at hand, a list was sent around to the various homes so that each person desiring to write might select a boy in whom he or she was particularly interested. Not being a teacher, matron, foreman or the like, I don't have an opportunity to know all the children here as well as I'd like to. Ever since we have been at the orphanage, however, there have been some who for one reason or another found their way to our house, when they were still children, and made themselves at home here. These we came to know and to regard as our own. And though some, like you, have been

200

away now for a good many years, we have never forgotten nor ceased to be interested in the welfare of each one.

I am sure that you will hear or have already heard from others at the orphanage, because you left many friends here and you have come back often since your graduation. But since you were perhaps the very first of the group I have mentioned, I want to write too. Perhaps there can't be too many to write and say how proud we are of you and the others now standing "between their loved land and the war's desolation."

Not that in your case our pride goes back only to the day, not so long ago, on which you first put on a uniform. You were always the kind of boy that institutions like to point out as proof of their superior methods of rearing children.

I must say that you picked a nice place in which to spend the winter. Still, it must be a hardship to forego autumn in North Carolina even for the climatic charms of Florida. The campus here is a glory of copper, bronze, wine-red and gold — yes, and there is still a lot of green left. The leaves have begun to fall but not really in earnest yet. Last year Daddy said our yard looked as though it were buried under a blanket of potato chips. Wouldn't it be nice if all the leaves would turn into potato chips as soon as they touched the ground — crisp, golden brown, and well salted?

But I'm perfectly willing for the chrysanthemums to stay just as they are without turning into anything else. I love every one of them — the starry white ones, the perky yellow ones, the big scraggly ones, the little button ones, the pink ones, the bronze ones — any and all of them.

Speaking of chrysanthemums reminds me of football and that reminds me that the orphanage team wound up its season Saturday with a 33-6 win over the Thomasville Bulldogs. The victory gave Mills Home a perfect con-

201

ference record of seven straight wins and no defeats. Ask your buddies how their hometown teams came out and see if any of them can beat yours. The only game dropped by the orphanage was the opening contest with High Point, which belongs to another league. You can imagine the elation of Coach Kearns and the boys.

Well, the associations are over, but the men representing the orphanage still continue on the go from now until Thanksgiving. The ladies here say they can't see any difference between this and any other year as far as the automobile situation is concerned: They are used to being afoot. But that fact doesn't keep a number of them from making the mile walk to town several times a week to roll bandages for the Red Cross. Remembering the amount of time an orphanage matron has to be on her feet in the fulfillment of her regular duties, you will agree, I think, that these women are doing their part.

Come to see us whenever you can. We shall miss many of you old boys at Christmas-time this year — for this letter is really to all of you — but we shall not forget. The old place will be ready to welcome you any time you can come back.

Until then, so long, and the best of luck to you!
Louise MacMillan

Suddenly the war was two years old. The troop trains continued to move uniformed men and women through town from one duty station to another or to a port of embarkation. Otherwise, the outward manifestations of war were few. There were, of course, women clad in slacks working jobs formerly held by men in furniture plants. Uniforms walking on city streets clothed Red Cross supervisors, service men and women on furlough, or those taking a few days delay en route to grab a barbecue sandwich or to see a girl.

The Sunday newspaper disturbed Sabbath calm by its very bulk and diverse contents. Column after column of war news, drawn from every portion of the globe, and supplemented with maps and pictures, depicted the gains, the losses, the distances covered, the distances still to go. Headlines read, "Yanks Advance Two Miles," "Heavy Fighting Continues," "Twenty-Seven Bombers Fail to Return."

Fathers brought their sons' letters to be published; they expressed the poignant hope that this awful thing not happen again. Editorials pointed with pride or viewed with alarm; couched always in dignified sober language that befitted the hour.

With such momentous news would there be room for anything else? Editors thought so. The same section that carried the soldier's letter to his father also carried articles on cooking, cosmetics, fashions in clothes, interior decoration, and postwar municipal planning.

Advertisers introduced the "More-hat" mood in black silk taffeta at $22.75, and silken suits — "Cool...yes, but as mannered and worldly as your most elegant woolens...at $29.95," and shoes, "Summer suedes so light and airy you expect a summer breeze to lift it...at $16.95 per pair."

People continued to marry and have children. Books continued to be reviewed, ranging from the deeply serious to the very light. And news from the worlds of music, art, science, and from the field of entertainment continued to be published.

The orphanage still went to sleep like a flock of sparrows noisily going to roost; shrill chattering dropping off little by little until only an occasional chirrup emanated from the Downing, Mitchell, West Chowan, Hutchinson, Watson, Mothers, and so on.

The big boys at Hutchinson always lingered on the steps, on the porch, at the door, waving across the valley to their girls at the Downing and Huffman. Sometimes the boys grouped and in good voice of zest serenaded the campus — sending out The Marine Hymn, then "Deep in the Heart of Texas." Then, in great spirit, they rendered "Send the Light" followed by fragments of boogie woogie. Finally, the current hit "Coming in on a Wing and a Prayer," or "Praise the Lord and Pass the Ammunition." They then gave the night over to the chorus of crickets and cicadas.

The cramp of shortages began to be felt. Vacations were

limited to those children whose families could come for them in private cars. Excursions in the farm truck were banned and travel on the highways dropped to 35 miles per hour by decree of Governor Broughton. New shoes were unavailable, and old shoes went unrepaired until Frank Bailey received a medical discharge from the Navy and reactivated the shoe shop. Soaping the bathroom floor to slide around while in the shower was no longer possible; soap was precious. Grease was at a premium and fatback unavailable.

The class of 1942, twenty-five in number, counted the days to graduation so they could take a crack at the WAVES, WAACS, SPARS, and Army and Navy.

Miss Wright's sewing room became the focal point for preparing Red Cross dressings as women from divergent groups gathered to fold 4x4's for hours at a stretch. They folded and listened and chatted. A woman's son, a chaplain, married to a Thomasville girl; was recently promoted from lieutenant to captain. Another had a son killed in action. Another's daughter, a nurse in North Africa, had written that she painted her new quarters, a hotel room, to make it habitable. And, babies crowded the conversation; who gained how many pounds, and who wanted a girl but would not give back the precious boy.

War stories about orphanage boys began arriving. Owen Koontz wrote that his plane was downed off the coast of Italy.

"We went out as usual on Sunday," Owen wrote, "I can't say how many ships were fighters or where we went besides Italy. We were coming in on the target and the flak was heavy. After we bombed the target we turned for home,, about 50 miles off the coast. Around 100 ME 109's hit us and our rudder and wing and engine were shot away. The engines were knocked out completely and at about 1,000 feet the ship caught on fire. Two of our gunners baled out. We landed in the ocean with the ship burning as merrily as you please. It was a good landing. We got out the life raft and were picked up that night none the worse for harm."

Woody Baldwin, also a fighter pilot in Italy, wrote that he had twelve flying missions to his credit; four of them having carried him deep into Germany. Earlier in the war, Woody had thrilled us by buzzing the campus in a P-51 that he picked up in Winston-Salem and flew to Abilene, Texas.

A letter about Johnnie Williams came from Dr. and Mrs. Carl Tyner, friends of the orphanage.

Dear Mr. Greer:

When we were fixing Christmas boxes for overseas we fixed an extra one or two and sent them "For Soldiers who do not receive boxes" and put them in care of the Chaplains of the particular "A.P.O." we were most interested in and sent them along with our boxes to family or friends. I'm sure you will be interested in the final destination of one of them.

In January my brother in France wrote us he received our boxes to him a week or so late and at the same time, for some reason we do not know, our box to his A.P.O. address for an "unknown soldier" was turned over to him for disposal. That seemed remarkable enough to us — and, he wrote that after a discussion with the mail clerk they decided to send it on to "an orphan boy who was at a lonely outpost" — and what seems even more remarkable is that the box should have gone to one of your boys — I'm sure you will be interested in having his letter.

We would have liked to have seen you and Mrs. Greer when you were here last week. We hear that you put on an exceptionally good program for the Carolina Council. Being, as Dr. Tyner insists on calling me, "A Mountain Gal" and having been "started off" in an atmosphere of folk songs and ballads and mountain superstitions I know what a good program it must have been; and too we always like to see you when you are close by.

Sincerely yours,
Charlotte B. Tyner

Johnnie replied to the Tyners' kindness.

Dear Dr. and Mrs. Tyner:

I had quite a surprise a few days ago and I wish to thank you very much for the surprise. It was a very pleasant surprise, I assure you. You are probably wondering who I am and what I am trying to say. My name is John M. Williams (Johnnie to you) and I am trying to thank you for the Christmas box that I received, addressed to "A soldier without a Christmas box." Yes, I am proud to say, I was the lucky one, and contrary to the law of average, your box found its way into the hands of a "Tar Heel." For we have very few N. C. boys compared to what we formerly had.

I might as well tell you a little about myself, too, while I am at it. I was born in Morganton, N. C. and I went to the Mills Home Orphanage in 1929. I was there for 11 years and incidentally I was on the baseball team there, and we played Leaksville a lot while I was there. I am 25 years old and have 4 years in the army and 29 months overseas. I have fought in Africa, Sicily, Italy (one year) and came to France a few days after the Southern Invasion. I think that covers most of it and if there is anything you would like to know I will be more than glad to tell you.

I suppose this will be enough for the time being, and I would like very much to hear from you, if you have time to write. Tell "Joe and Ann" hello for me and give them my best regards. So thanks again for the Christmas box and I sincerely hope all of you had a nice Christmas and New Year.

Sincerely yours,
Johnnie Williams

A letter came about Barney Smith:
Mr. Cyrus M. Howell
Mills Home
Thomasville, N.C.

Dear Mr. Howell:

I am enclosing a little bit of news about Barney Smith who is a Sergeant in the South Pacific.

It came to me from one of the boys, Sgt. James M. Horne, who is a member of our church and who met Barney on one of the Islands.

Quote: "I ran into a very interesting fellow when we first hit this Island. He is Sgt. Barney Smith of High Point, N. C. He was at Mills Home. He was quite a hero out here. Got 43 Japs in one night. So far as I know that's a record. At any rate, it was for here. He is a fine fellow.

I thought perhaps you would like to have this for your column, which I enjoy each week.

Best wishes to all the "Old Timers" who remember me.

Sincerely yours,
Elsie Denny

Frank Bailey wrote an open letter to all service men and women, bringing them up to date on orphanage life.

Hi Fellows:

I'm writing you this open letter because so many of you, in your letters to me, want to know how things are at the Mills Home.

The big thing at present is the restrictions put on all young people throughout North Carolina because of the Polio situation. We can remember how penned up we felt back in 1937 when we had a case here on the campus. It's not that bad now for we have had no cases; but the kids here feel it just the same. They can't go to the "cowboys" on Saturday afternoon or look across the church on Sunday and wink at the girl-friend. They, the children, are lucky though, for there is swimming in the old pool at the foot of the hill, visiting the girl-friend on Sunday afternoons, and outdoor church services on the hill between the sewing room and the infirmary. You can see it's not so bad.

The ball club that you fellows are so interested in hasn't formed yet. Mr. Skaggs can't seem to find a coach. The prospects are pretty "skimpy" too, although I think we should have a pretty fair first team. When football is mentioned by some of the boys here they start the ball rolling with me. They hear first hand what a good kicker Carl Watson was, how tough Roy Chatham was at guard, why Joe Hawkins made All-State, and of course what a team Mills Home lost when the class of '39 finished — nine first team men lost, the best being Pat Preston.

All of you write for addresses of boys from here, but I can't put them in this letter — Uncle Sam has his censors for papers too. We have classmates, schoolmates and friends all over the world. Wherever there's a fight for freedom or a scrap with a bully, there you will find a boy from the Mills Home. There isn't a place anywhere on the globe that you can't find a former Mills Home boy. We have lost four so far, and they have all gone down fighting. That goes to show you what kind of guys we have in the service — all four killed in the service — all four killed in action!

Well, in answer to your question, "Is there anybody there we know?", I shall say, "a few." Mr. McKoin is still running his farm satisfactorily; Paul Edinger still holds the rate of foreman on the farm; "Doc" Early still raises darn good friers and is handy man in general; Miss Carter still holds down the Watson house; Miss Hester, whom you younger ones remember, is still the right arm at the Mothers; Mrs. T. H. Hilliard, who you all remember, is now matron at the Chowan; Mrs. Frazier and Mrs. Barbee are still on the first team at the Green building; Miss Faircloth is still at the Whitty; Mrs. Nipper, without her dog Penny, still keeps the Biggs house in line; Mrs. Garret, who used to be at the Watson house to cook your meals, is at the Mitchell; Mrs. G. W. Edwards, of Hutchinson building fame is at the Downing; Mrs. Britton of the W. C. B., has moved up to the new building beside of Mr. McMillan's, known as the Huffman; still serving in the positions as you remember them are: Mr. Neilson, Mr. McMillan, Miss Sallie, Mr. Greer, Mr. Covington, Mr. Millsaps, Miss Edwards, Miss Elmore — our new superintendent, Miss Council, Miss Olive, Mr. Skaggs, Mr. Lord, Mrs. Crump, Miss Sherman, Mrs. Wright, and Mr. Harmon. You night owls remember "old Bob." I about forgot Ferd Gaily, Kirk Louya, and the print shop force, which still consists of Cy Howell, Ted Hethcock and Tom Whitley. I think you all know where I work. If you have forgotten let me quote Jackson Coley, a classmate of mine, "He mends and saves more soles than the preacher.

Now fellows, you can easily see the old home is essentially the same. You will find there has been a new building put up, but away down deep the Mills Home's heart beats just as it did when we were growing up here. Personally I found her worth fighting for and so have you!

Until that great day of peace when we can hold that great big "bull session" here on the old campus, I'll say so long.

Your friend,
C. F. "Frank" Bailey

It happened countless times, as warships took aboard new men for transport or as crew, as new men arrived on a new base, at liberty ports; orphanage boys found other orphanage boys.

George Bailey, aboard the Roe, had the fantail watch from four until eight o'clock while anchored in San Juan. They had taken aboard fifty recruits newly arrived from boot camp in Norfolk. The new men were stretched out on deck. George saw a familiar name on a recruit's pillowcase. He woke him up. It was James Allen VanLandingham, another orphanage boy.

Maurice Owen became a champion boxer in the 125 pound class of the Desert Training Camp in California. He stepped into the ring to fight a scheduled bout and faced Spurgeon Whiteside, another orphanage boy. They fought to a draw. They then talked over old days. Both went on to win championships after that.

I met Poogie Clement on the U.S.S. Missouri when I was in boot camp in Norfolk. Cal went to Philadelphia while in radio school at Bainbridge to see Pat Preston play for Duke against Navy in football. Afterwards they visited and talked over the old days. Don Harrelson met Reece Gardner and Bobby and Harry Thompson at boot camp in San Diego and John Beach in Japan.

There were countless designed as well as undesigned get togethers around the world; more than we have space to recount. Whenever we met we celebrated our similarities, reverting to orphanage teachings and mores, told our stories, and relived our days. In this way we singled ourselves out of the (to us) undifferentiated mass of Americans. We were not totally resistant to national homogeneity but we were decidedly clannish. But, as for being Americans; we were perhaps the Quintessential American; self-confident, patriotic, religious, happy, and exuding vitality.

During this period I became interested in girls but, being shy, was of no danger to anyone. Big orphanage boys told middle-sized boys things about sex that struck our ears as being so preposterous that we rejected them out of hand. My own adoration was silent, even sullen, because I was afraid of girls and went to considerable effort to avoid contact. But, I mooned away at heart's content at the endless parade of pretty orphanage girls who passed through days of school, duty, church, and sports. My fear of girls did nothing to dampen an active imagination that spent triumphant days and nights in pursuit as well as in fulfillment. The girls in my class at school were pals. They could always be counted on to explain the mysteries of geometry.

My days of watching the opposite sex from a yearning distance came to an end when Gilbert Byrd told me that Frances Edinger liked me and wanted me to come sit in her porch swing. Oh I knew Fran. I had pushed her down the steps on the way to music class in the sixth grade and Mr. Lord had humiliated me by whipping me with my own belt. But, I accepted the invitation, not realizing the portent there was in that one move. For a year we two sat together in the swing on Sunday afternoon while Gilbert lounged around on the porch rail.

It was during this time that the grandest social event for seasons was held on the campus; Miss Fan Bost, our likable social services teacher, announced that she was to be married. Fran was chosen as one of the bridesmaids, and, dressed in pastel taffeta and carrying nosegays, stood at the foot of the choir loft and sang love songs. I was an usher.

The event sparked a turning point in life as I knew it. I told Fran to wait on her front porch after church, the Sunday night following the wedding. I was on kitchen duty at the Watson, charged to replenish the coal scuttle and the kindling box before bedtime. Fran waited. I could see her in the shadows. As I went to the coal shed I put down the shuttle and took off to join her. It was not a lingering, only a brief moment, time enough to clumsily kiss her, our first. I tasted only half her lips but the sensation was so exquisite I almost fell off the porch.

It was not like a mother's kiss, with dryness, a touching of the cheek or forehead, nor was it a peck as when Aunt Gus kissed, like a chicken pecking corn from the ground.

The softness of Fran's mouth was a glory of surprise, cool and with an easy patina of moisture. After that, had Miss Carter no other charge than I, and a hundred eyes, and ten ears, she could have spent all her waking and half her sleeping hours and still not been able to keep me from Fran's front porch.

The struggle between Miss Carter and me began. I slept in the ground floor dormitory and the windows faced the road that ran between the Watson Cottage and Mr. Paul's house. Every evening as dark fell I was out the window to Fran's. I could see into the cottage windows and hear the cottage sounds from Fran's porch. Miss Carter roamed, looking for me. "Ted Chandler," she called, peering into the empty dormitory. She went to the front porch, then to the back porch, "Ted Chandler," she yelled. By that time I had returned through the window and, stripping off my shirt and shoes, sat in the chair next to the door, opened the door and called out to Miss Carter, "You looking for me, Miss Carter?"

"Where have you been?" she asked.

"Right here, getting ready for bed," I lied.

The following morning she nailed the screen closed and that evening I pried it loose. From that point it was parry and thrust, tactic and counter. The ruses became more shrewd if not devious. Wild horses could not keep me away.

Time passed. The class of 1945 practiced long and presented "The Home Fronters" as senior play to two overflow audiences. By this time my punishment for sneaking off to the movie with Fran was over and I was allowed to participate. I played Andy Tefler, a likable lad. The other festivities of graduation were scheduled as before the war; the junior-senior reception, Baccalaureate sermon, the band concert, but the war had cut our number to thirteen.

Our class contributed these to the war:

George Breedlove, Navy	Paul Justice, Navy;
David Dula, Navy;	Erskine Johnson, Navy;
Everette Frye, Army	James McDonald, Army;
Van Hall, Navy;	Wilbur Noel, Navy;
Carroll Hartley, Marines;	Thomas Snead, Navy;
Leonard Helms, Army;	William Tucker, Navy.
Ralph Hill, Navy;	

When I graduated that June day in 1945 the end of the war was yet two months away. Three hundred twelve of our best fought, these were killed in action:

Clifton Benton	James B. Norville
Virgil Briles	Clyde V. Owens
Edgar J. Green	William D. Ross
Alford Haire	Wilbur Spaul
Lucian Malpass	Bennie Thomas

Defending our country in war seemed natural to us. We responded and gave whatever was demanded of us, to achieve the victory.

Fran.

ROLL OF HONOR

ROBERT BASS
HORACE BOYETTE
ELWOOD CRAFT
CHARLES HESTER
HARVEY HILL
BILLY HOLMES
HARRY HUBBARD
ALLEN JONES
MELVIN JONES
ODELL JONES
CLIFTON LANGLEY
J.R.LAWS
ROBERT LAWS
JAMES.H.LOWE
LUCIAN MALPASS
CHARLES MEDFORD

DONALD A.MOORE
CLARENCE MEDFORD
DAVID McKEE
JAMES M.McKEE
CALVIN RICHARDSON
WILLIAM D ROSS
DEAVER SHELL
LUTHER SUTHERS
CARL SYDES
RCHARD SYDES
CARLTON WEATHERINGTON
EARL WESTER
COY WHITMAN
MARION J.WHITMAN
HERBERT WOMBLE
WILLIAM HAITHCOCK

FRANKLIN BAILEY	CLAUDE BATES	LYNN HAMMOND	RICHARD MITCHELL	GRADY THOMAS	WILLIAM FISHER
NELSON BAILEY	TOM COATES	REECE HARRIS	JULIAN MITCHELL	FRED THOMPSON	CHARLES GODWIN
GEORGE BAILEY	SAM DAY	HAROLD HAYNIE	CURTIS OWEN	ALEX TYSINGER	JOHN GODWIN
WOODROW BALDWIN	CARL DAY	J.B.HAYNIE	MAURICE OWEN	WILLIAM VESTER	LUTHER GRAY
ROBERT BEASLEY	OBED DAY	TED HARMOND	RAYMOND PEELER	HARVEY WALLS	BILL HOLDFIELD
SAM BRADLEY	SAM DOTSON	GORDON HARRISON	ROBERT PEELER	LAWRENCE WATSON	ED HOWIE
GROVER BRADSHAW	JAKE DOTSON	JAMES HARRINGTON	VERNON BRADY	CARL WATSON	GUY HILL
ANDREW BRIDGES	CAROL DODD	ALFRED HAIRE	ROBERT POPLIN	HAROLD WARREN	ERNEST HAYNIE
CHARLIE BRIDGES	CLAY FOX	JOE HAWKINS	RALPH POUNDERS	CHARLES WALTON	TYSON KIRK
EDGAR BRIDGES	JACK FAIRES	PERCY HENRY	GAITHER PRESTON	LUTHER WHETSTINE	PARKER McDANIEL
HOWARD BROWN	J.W.FRANK	WILLIAM HOCKADAY	ERNEST PRICE	SPURGEON WHITESIDES	MONROE MILLER
JOHN.L.BYERLY	WILL FROST	ROBERT HOCKADAY	WARREN PRICE	HOBERT WILSON	PAT PRESTON
HINIARD BORDEAUX	JOE HOBSON	CLARENCE W.HODGES	DOUGLAS PROCTOR	JOHNNY WILLIAMS	EUGENE ROLLINS
RONALD BAREFOOT	ERNEST HILL	LOY HUNSUCKER	ROBERT PULLIAM	EDGAR.J.GREENE	AnRON SPAUL
RAYMOND V.BUCKNER	LEE HOOD	LARRY HUMPHRIES	JOHNNY RATLEDGE	JAMES.B.NORVILLE	CARL SHAVER
MARION J.BUCKNER	JAY LEE JONES	ROBERT HONEYCUTT	CLAUDE RHYNE	JAMES CLAYTON	WILLIAM TUCKER
HUDSON CASWELL	OWEN KOONTZ	YOUNG HOWARD	DAVID RITCHIE	JOE BRADY	GARLAND WILLIAMS
MARGARETT CAMDEN	BEN OAKLEY	WESLEY HOWARD	LEE RAY ROSS	S.WILKIE CRAVER Jr	CHRIS CREECH
ROY CHATHAM	JOE PHELPS	ROBERT JACKSON	CLARENCE SHAVER	FRANK POE	GIBBS MOORE
ROGER CARROLL	COLEY REID	BELVIN JACKSON	HAROLD SHAVER	MYRTLE COOPER	ROBERT BELCH
RICHARD CLAYWELL	GUY RITCHIE	JESSE JARRELL	JAMES.S.SHORE	CLEGG BARBEE	LESTER LAWS
TROY CRAWFORD	ALEX ROSS	ERNEST.L.JOHNSON	JAMES SMITH	ROBERT ALEXANDER	RICHARD PERDUE
ROBERT CARROLL	ROSS SOWERS	DOUGLAS KOONTS	WASHINGTON SEARS	GEORGE AYERS	JOHN ANDERSON
JAMES CRUMPLER	OSCAR SOWERS	JEP LEIGHTON	WILBUR SPAUL	ROY BOWERS	BOYDEN McGUIRE
JACKSON COLEY	JESSIE TILLEY	WILLARD LESTER	WILLIE SPAUL	TOM CLAYTON	ROY McGUIRE
ROBERT DOYLE	OTIS WALLS	THOMAS LLOYD	BEMBERT SWARINGER	CALVIN CHANDLER	BEN ABERNATHY
EDWARD M.DUNCAN	TED WARREN	NATHANIEL LLOYD	ROLAND SWINK	ROBERT CLEMENT	JAMES ABERNATHY
RALPH DUNCAN	ROBERT WHITT	J.VAN LANDINGHAM	WORTH SWINK	LEWIS DAY	HIRAM ATKINSON
BEULAH FARMER	IVA WEST	HAROLD MARLETTE	ROBERT TAYLOR	RAY EVANS	EARL BAILEY
LEE FOWLER	DWIGHT WEST	VERNON McLEAN	ED THOMAS	ROBERT EDWARDS	HALLIE BISHOP
CLIFFORD FOX	JUDY WOODS	HAROLD MITCHELL	GROVER THOMAS	CHARLES ELMORE	ROBERT.N.BAREFOOT

Armed Forces Roll of Honor.

16

Equipping the Mind

D id it work? Did this grandly simple design for nurturing the intellectual, physical, and moral vigor of children produce adults who lived fulfilling and useful lives? Did the tireless and sacrificial investment of love and labor by matrons, teachers, supervisors, and administrators equip their young charges with competence, self-confidence,and compassion to respond to life's variable challenges, including the kinds of human needs the orphanage itself was created to meet?

A resounding yes to these questions came forth from the record of what orphanage alumni have done with their lives as citizens, family members, church members, and practitioners of a great variety of professions and trades.

We left the orphanage imbued with certain foundational convictions: faith in God as revealed in Jesus Christ, love of country, and a sense of ourselves as God's stewards of whatever resources of talent, opportunity, and wealth came into our possession. These bedrock convictions were not the apex of our development but rather the foundation on which we would build the superstructure of our lives. As we left we were still in a state of becoming, and the differences among us signaled clearly that we would follow many paths to fulfillment and usefulness.

There was the reality of inherent differences. John couldn't drive a nail without mashing his thumb while Cal could do anything with a set of tools. I was somewhere between. Differences in assigned duties added to the variety of talents and shaping influences. The barn and farm boys learned to milk, drive a tractor, gather hay, thresh grain, plant corn. The print shop boys ran presses, dabbed printer's ink, and operated linotype machines. The sewing room girls cut out and stitched cloth and ran sewing machines. The laundry girls ran mangles, presses, and irons. The girls at the infirmary cared for the sick. In some instances our experiences with a duty deterred us from that vocational path. Relatively few who worked at the dairy or on the farm chose those activities for their life's work.

Our education was broad based. We were introduced to the romantic poets by Miss Myra Olive, to historical perspectives and geographical possibilities by Miss Fan Bost, and I learned French syntax from Miss Louise McMillan. We were taught practical things; typing, shorthand, agriculture, and home economics. As we progressed through high school our teachers expected all of us to follow a particular curricular plan: college preparation for some, vocational training for others. As we left each of us had a job and a plan to begin life outside.

Some graduates of the early years of the orphanage became leading business figures in North Carolina, South Carolina, and Virginia. Those who followed became publishers of newspapers, printers, nurses, teachers, lawyers, dentists, preachers, farmers, draftsmen, school principals, judges, high school and college educators, social workers, musicians, physicians, wives of community leaders.

In 1945 my class joined the alumni ranks. A total of about 4,000 graduates had passed through the orphanage and were known to be living in 24 states, Cuba, and the Canal Zone. Additionally, those in the armed forces were spread round the world.

Our roots were in the orphanage and the memories of how

it looked, smelled, and sounded gave us serenity. There was something in those sensations that was as vital to us as a home slope was for a Douglas fir. Our affinity for this place was expressed in nostalgia. Nostalgia was manifested in gratitude and anticipation. This letter came from nine alumni living in the same boarding house:

Dear Cy:

We are enthusiastically looking forward to the great day when we shall be together on Home-Coming to see our brothers and sisters.

To begin with, there are nine of us alumni living here in the same boarding house, so you can depend on all of us being at Home-Coming. Of all the old graduates that have left in past years, I don't think you can find that many anywhere in North Carolina who are living under the same roof.

We also wish to invite all alumni up to spend any weekend that is convenient to suit them.

We are all employed and getting along just fine with our work.

Tell all of our friends and loved ones we are thinking and praying for them always.

Looking forward to that great day, we are sincerely and earnestly looking forward to having a grand time.

As ever your friends, .
    John Randall Whitt
    Andrew Bridges
    Joe Brady
    Larry Humphries
    Wilbur Spaul
    Edgar Bridges
    William Frost
    Harvey Wall
    J. W. Frank

This letter came from an orphanage boy:

I am working. Just a job till I get something better. This is my first check. I couldn't think of anything better than to send it to the Mills Home. I have been very lonesome and homesick. I miss Mills Home more than I thought I would. I didn't ever think I would appreciate what has been done for me there so much. I appreciate Mills Home and all the teachers and workers.

P. S. Miss Olive did her best to teach me to express myself in writing, but I don't show any of my teaching in this letter.

Dick Mitchell, aboard the USS Leary, sent a letter at Christmas and the following books:

Krey — "On the Long Tide"
Emerson — "Essays"
Macy — "The Story of the World's Literature"
Daniels — "A Southerner Discovers New England"
Longfellow — "The Poems of Longfellow"
Dixon — "The Human Side of Birds"
Meigs — "Vanished Island"
Lay — "I Wanted Wings"
Partridge — "A Lady Goes to Hollywood"
Hess — "Buckaroo"
Hess — "Leather Pants"
Holbrook — "Tall Timber"
Dwight — "Kentucky Cargo"

Casey Medlin wrote from Baltimore:

I have work now, and am enclosing $2.00 for the Mills Home. I thought since it is the first money I have earned that it was only right to send it. For the Mills Home has made it possible for me to be where I am today. It is not much but I have just secured work.

Johnny Allen wrote:

Dear Mr. Greer:

I am sending the boys, under separate cover, a catcher's mitt, and hope that with such a mitt Mills Home will produce a Major League Catcher. I know it is rather late for baseball equipment, but I received the mitt only this week from the factory, and thought I had better entrust it to you rather than take a chance on sending it along in the spring.

With sincere kind regards.

Yours very truly,
Johnny Allen.

Inez Patterson wrote:

Dear Mr. Covington:

With a heart full of love and gratitude, I'm sending this dollar as my Thanksgiving offering to you. I wish I were able to send more, because I understand what Thanksgiving means to Mills Home.

I think of you all every day, and I hope every one is well and happy.

Yours sincerely,
Inez Patterson.

Graduates' letters revealed the yearning for community; this was lost upon leaving the orphanage. Loneliness was evident. The girls felt this more strongly for they had little exposure to the outside before graduation. For years we lived in cottages with thirty-five other boys or girls and among workers and teachers who prodded our minds into action, tolerated stupid error, encouraged fun, laughter, and getting together, and promoted robust individuality. At the same time they set down rules of behavior that were designed to keep the community together. Above everything community was required. On the outside the sense of loss of community was acute. The antidote for reentry into the world was the creation of another community. Some of us

219

did this by going to college, others got jobs, some joined the armed forces, others married or joined a church. Always we were searching for that which we had lost. And, we looked forward to recapturing that which we had lost by attending homecoming.

From one year to the next we lived in anticipation of homecoming, the first weekend in August. Throughout the year, wherever we were, we looked for the *Charity and Children* in the mail each week and straightway turned to the "Alumni News." Of course, some of the news was about graduates who had come and gone before our day. But old timers searched the column just as assiduously as we because invariably there occurred a name they hadn't seen for five, ten, fifteen, twenty, or thirty years, and suddenly they were yielded a flash out of the past, so vivid that for an instant they were young again.

Homecoming, a time of ball games, watermelon feasts, lemonade, and fellowship, was attended each year by about fifteen hundred, including families. They returned to be among those with whom they grew up; those with whom they shared common experiences and common memories. But the best thing about homecoming was the sheer pleasure it brought to everyone; the pleasure in talking over old times. Homecoming was a renewal of community.

I know of only one orphanage boy who went to prison. It was around 1913. He was released in 1933 and wrote Mr. Greer a letter expressing regret that he had let the orphanage and himself down. Mr. Greer responded with a letter of encouragement. One year later another letter came to Mr. Greer. The man was desperate. He had no job, no place to live, no money. He saw no way other than a return to crime.

Mr. Greer located an alumnus who owned a business and was assured that the former prison inmate would not only be given a job but could stay in the house of the alumnus. Mr. Greer went for the man and delivered him to the job and home. A year later Mr. Greer heard from the wife of the alumnus. The man was not only doing well in his work but was a gentleman in the home.

I left the orphanage in June 1945. At that time Cal was on patrol in the North Atlantic and John, majoring in Greek and English, was about to finish at Wake Forest. John garnered honors by the score; Phi Beta Kappa, Omicron Delta Kappa, Who's Who in Colleges and Universities, vice-president of the senior class, president of the Baptist Student Union, president of the Euzelian Literary Society; member of Eta Sigma Phi, classical language fraternity, and member of the International Relations Club.

I packed my trunk, collected the balance of my senior pay, about five bucks if I remember accurately, and headed to High Point where I had a job at Gibson's Ice Cream Company. Leonard Evans also had a job at Gibson's and we roomed together in a private home with a sweet woman whose only complaint was that our aim was imperfect when we stood at the commode. Mr. Gibson, owner of The Company, was one of my clothing people and he was anxious that I pass muster during the summer so that he could send me in the fall to State College to be educated in dairy production.

Work was accepted as inevitable. Since my days with Miss Ballard I had learned that if you don't work you don't eat. Still, I was frustrated. Smouldering in my mind was the idea of being a doctor but it was no unquenchable flame. By nature I was lazy and had the temperament of a wanderer.

At Gibson's my job was to operate the pasteurizer. For 35 cents an hour I rolled ten-gallon coolers of milk from the freezers and with a helper heaved them up and dumped the contents into a giant stainless cauldron. I twirled a few controls and let the milk bubble to the boiling point as indicated by a metal stylus on a revolving disc. When the boiling ended I cut the heat and opened valves to sluice the steamed contents to the top of a large corrugated iron cooling screen. The milk ran down the screen and then, having cooled off considerably, it coursed through a pipe to ice cream mixing vats.

I tried to generate enthusiasm for the work, but Leonard left for the Navy before the first month was out, creating a loneliness in me. The change from living with 35 in a cottage to living by myself was tough. There was some slight chance I might have stuck it out had I not incurred the justifiable wrath of Kellar, the foreman. I omitted a crucial step one morning when I failed to cap the outflow pipe at the bottom of the cooler, creating a grand mess and quite a stir as the velvety milk carpeted the floor. I wasn't fired, but an excuse to quit was inviting. So I packed my trunk, put it on the bus to Aunt Gus's and hit the road, my thumb out. I headed for Thomasville to see Fran, then to Black Mountain to see Mama, Aunt Gus, and B. H. and then to Atlanta to enlist in the Merchant Marines, a choice inspired by my yearning to see the world.

After a few hours with Fran I caught a ride with an overly friendly gentleman whose large hand rested uncomfortably on my leg. He was only going to Salisbury but it was dark when we arrived and he, knowing well that I had no other place to go, invited me to spend the night with him. I declined and spent the night on the road. By nightfall of the next day I was in Black Mountain and before heading to Atlanta spent a few days eating Aunt Gus's biscuits and visiting around.

The day I left for Atlanta I caught a ride with two jovial mountain boys who regularly reached into the glove compartment to pull out a liquor bottle, swig from it and pass it on, all the while taking mountain curves on two wheels. They stopped to refuel, pouring gasoline from a tin can that had sloshed into the trunk and dripped onto the exhaust pipe. The boy on the passenger's side kept insisting that I share the bottle, shoving it into the back seat. I took it and returned it without drinking. The more he drank the nastier he got. Upon reaching Murphy I counted myself fortunate to still be living and declared to them my intention to layover in town for the night. We parted company.

The remaining rides on the way to Atlanta were quite ordinary and upon arriving I found the Merchant Marine recruiting office and stood in line to sign up as an able-bodied seaman. There had been confusion as to my name at the orphanage. On the rolls I was listed as Theodore Roosevelt Chandler. But Aunt Gus insisted that Theodore Roosevelt wasn't correct, for she named me herself. In Atlanta I believed my name to be Theodore Roosevelt and signed up under that name. I was told that as soon as I obtained a birth certificate I could enter training at Sheepshead Bay, New York.

I didn't linger. Back to the road; destination, the town of Marshall, county seat of Madison County. In Marshall I asked the Register of Deeds for a copy of a birth certificate for Theodore Roosevelt Chandler born December 27, 1927. He found no such entry.

I suggested that he look under Baxter Harrison and Mamie Chandler. He found the name of Edgar Ted Chandler. I paid the $1.00 fee, went to the dime store, bought a bottle of ink eradicator and removed the Edgar Ted, replacing it with Theodore Roosevelt, mailed the document and headed to Aunt Gus's to await the call.

The Merchant Marine officer wrote, "It appears, sir, that this document has been altered, an offense punishable by law." I chucked the letter and with it went my hope of life on the high seas.

I spent a summer of aimless days in Black Mountain and as fall approached enrolled at Mars Hill College, borrowing $125.00 from the orphanage education fund. The war was over. Cal returned to Black Mountain and got work as registrations clerk at the Moore General Veteran's Hospital. John was in graduate school at Duke.

At Mars Hill I whiled time away, performing abysmally and twinging when a professor said, "Oh you're John's brother." There were several orphanage girls and they were company but my mind was on Fran. Her front porch was miles away. On the weekends I hit the road to the orphanage, returning barely in time to make classes on Mondays.

Christmas holidays came. I was close to failing every course. I headed for the orphanage and stayed at the Watson cottage until sickness struck. Both ears became infected. Mr. Neilson took me into his home. Fran, Beverly Neilson, and Mrs. Neilson nursed me through days of high fever. Mr. Neilson called Dr. Furman Covington, who had just returned from service. I had no money but Dr. Covington came and gave me an injection of penicillin, which had just become available to civilians. I began healing when both eardrums ruptured from the pressure and drained. When I was able to return to Mars Hill it was the middle of January and exams were in progress.

It was hopeless. I went to the office of "Daddy" Blackwell, the president, and told him that I was withdrawing. He asked me to stay on. I said no and packed my trunk and sent it to Aunt Gus's. I went to the Navy recruiting station in Asheville. The corpsman examining me asked, "How long have you had trouble with your ears?"

"Never," I answered.

On February 9 I was in Raleigh, sworn in, and in a few days on my way to Norfolk to boot camp.

The discipline, barracks life, and regularity of the Navy were similar to orphanage life and I took to them straightway. I had joined up to become a hospital corpsman. In the recesses of my mind the idea of becoming a doctor was still alive. But, I was erratic in performance; scoring high in tests, doing poorly in course work, scoring high on the rifle range. It seemed not to be a matter of intellect or of confidence but of will. I was lazy.

I scored high enough on tests to qualify as a candidate for the Naval Academy Preparatory School but rejected the opportunity. After boot camp I went to Hospital Corps school, Bainbridge, Maryland, and from there was assigned to the Sampson Naval Hospital in upper New York State. During Corps school I had thumbed to the orphanage to see Fran a number of times.

At Sampson I served on the wards for awhile but landed in the scullery, the area where food trays were slopped and washed and garbage carried out. The scullery was usually staffed with sailors under punishment for breaking rules. To my knowledge I had not been caught breaking any. My friends passed through the line. "What are you doing in there?" they asked.

"Beats me," I answered.

One of my friends was a Brooklyn boy, Pete Pedersen. Pete was planning to go to medical school when he finished his Navy tour but for the moment he pushed a chow cart from the kitchen to the wards and ladled chow three times daily. He was not happy.

"I'm getting out of this," he said.

"How," I asked.

"They're going to take out my appendix this afternoon," he

said.

That afternoon at 3 o'clock he was in the operating room and his appendix was removed. While recovering from surgery, Pete was assigned to the laboratory under Dr. Jameson, the pathologist. Pete came to see me.

"I've got you a job in the lab," he said, "But you've got to have your appendix taken out."

He described the symptoms of appendicitis. I feigned sickness, vomiting, dizzying around, clutching my stomach, wretching in misery. I reported to sick bay. Dr. Jameson, the pathologist, was on duty. He diagnosed catarrhal fever and admitted me to the hospital for observation. I remained in the hospital a week and upon discharge, as promised, Pete had it rigged for me to get the laboratory job.

I was assigned as assistant to Lieutenant Wilma Funk, a wave officer in charge of bacteriology. Sampson was a hospital for sailors and veterans with tuberculosis and Lieutenant Funk began teaching me the techniques of searching slides for TB germs, of making culture media, and of culturing sputa.

A new world opened up. I absorbed the new information like a sponge and took to medical terms as though born to them. Many of the sailors in the laboratory planned to become doctors upon release. We became friends. On weekends we thumbed around. I didn't know much. They knew a lot. They introduced me to the region; Syracuse, Rochester, Geneva, Ithaca, Binghampton, New York City. They introduced me to taverns. They introduced me to girls. I did not see Fran during this time but we wrote regularly.

In February, 1947, Sampson was transferred to the Veteran's Administration and my friends and I were shipped out, many to the Naval hospital at St. Albans on Long Island, others to other places around the country. I had become proficient in bacteriology and was assigned to a research project studying streptomycin, a new drug for tuberculosis.

My new station was the Naval hospital at Corona, California, but before reporting I had five days delay en route and rode the train to Thomasville to see Fran.

225

The day after arrival Fran said, "I told Daddy that we were going to get married."

"I don't have any money," I said.

"It won't take much," she said.

I wired Dr. Jameson for $40.00. He sent it. Fran's mother and the matrons decorated the orphanage church. I wired John to be best man. At this time he was teaching at Wake Forest and pursuing a Ph.D. in philosophy at Duke. He roared into town "Where is that crazy fool?" he asked.

The arrangements took form and on Saturday we married before Fran's Uncle Clyde, a preacher. We took a taxi to the Sheraton Hotel in High Point and spent 24 hours of ignorant bliss. On Monday Fran returned to high school and I took the day coach to California.

Fran, accompanied on the trip by her sister Lois, came to California in June after Fran finished high school. We moved into a one room lodging with kitchen privileges rented from a woman who hated southerners. A hairless recluse was the other renter. We settled into housekeeping and had a good time stretching the money and learning about each other.

At work I was assigned to Commander Dorothy Oberon, who taught me specialized research techniques and encouraged me to consider medical school.

Fran remained in California until October and then returned home to live with her family. In December I was discharged. I wired my severance pay to Fran, except for $25.00, and hit the road, getting long rides to Tucson, El Paso, Fort Worth, Shreveport, and finally to Waynesville. In five days I was home and received by Mr. Paul and his family as though I were their own.

I went to work with a construction company that was building the freezer locker plant on the orphanage campus. But the foreman was not happy with my skill at sawing boards. "I don't believe this is your line of work," he said.

I agreed. And besides, the weather was bitter cold. I asked Mr. Paul if he could give me a job until I could find something more permanent. I only planned to work until I could enter Wake Forest in the fall. Mr. Paul placed me with Uncle Tom Thompson, clearing out the cattle sleeping barn. Uncle Tom and I forked manure all day. He was 75 years old and worked like a machine. "Don't work fast," he said, "Slow and easy gets the job done." He worked me to death. At the end of the first week I had thirty blisters on my hands.

Soon I had a job at Stroupe Mirror Company, cleaning mirrors. After about three months I moved for more money to plant D of the Thomasville Chair Company to work on the loading dock. Each of these jobs convinced me that, finally, the plan to enter college was the correct track.

John was awarded his Ph.D. from Duke and did additional graduate work at Harvard. He remained on the Wake Forest faculty for a few years and then joined the faculty of Williams College in Massachusetts. After several years at Williams he became president of Hamilton College in New York State and after five years at Hamilton returned to Williams as President. He led Williams in a distinguished way to a position of educational eminence and after twelve years as head became president of the Association of American Colleges in Washington. He remains its head at this writing.

I graduated from Wake Forest in 1951 and was admitted to medical school at the University of North Carolina, Chapel Hill. I had applied for and was granted a place as one of the first class of Morehead Scholars at the University. After leaving the university with my M.D. in 1955, I received additional training at the Baptist Hospital in Winston-Salem. I practiced medicine in Hickory for 18 years, and for the past 14 years I have directed the Adult Medicine Clinic at Reynolds Health Center and taught internal medicine at Wake Forest University's Bowman Gray School of Medicine.

Cal retired from directing hospitals, vowing to never sit behind another desk. He kept his word and is quite happy using his hands volunteering to build ramps onto houses of older infirm citizens. He's every bit as good at this as he was at leading hospitals.

Fran and I now live in Thomasville, in her parents' homeplace. On nice evenings we drive over to the orphanage and walk down the farm road, cross over Hamby's creek, curve around the knoll where I plowed new ground and continue on between Roses field and Long field. A freeway runs through part of the farm now and I never see children playing there. They go off campus to work and to school and can date at will and even own automobiles. They are not insulated from the real world the way we were.

Few of the children are orphans. Most have been removed from unstable homes by the courts or by social service departments and are in the home as wards of these agencies. Consequently, it is called a children's home, not an orphanage, except by those of us who lived there years ago. But the model is still the same, after 105 years the individual is the focus of effort and attention but community is required of all. In this I take hope, wishing that those millions of children who have unfit parents could have the opportunity I had, of growing up in an orphanage.

John, Cal, and I still attend the homecoming of old boys and girls every August, always with mixed pleasure and pain. We laugh with our friends about funny things that happened and are sad that so and so died during the year.

After all, the world can ill afford to lose us. We are samples of the reality of America. Not many of us were earth shakers but, on the other hand, when up against it we were not likely to collapse and vanish overnight. As long as this republic has people like us it will possess reserves of calm common sense that will enable it to continue to struggle with the tumultuous problems that beset her.

The End

Fran and Ted on their wedding day.

Homecoming.

Homecoming.